MIRACLES OF CHRISTMAS

Miracles of Christmas

Harold Shaw Publishers
Wheaton, Illinois

copyright © 1997 by Harold Shaw Publishers

ISBN 0-87788-563-X

Compiled by Miriam Mindeman
Cover design by David LaPlaca

Library of Congress Cataloging-in-Publication Data

Miracles of Christmas : stories by Katherine Paterson, Agatha Christie, Pearl S. Buck,
    Elizabeth Goudge & others.
        p.   cm.
    ISBN 0-87788-563-X
    1. Christmas stories, American. 2. Christmas stories, English. I. Paterson,
Katherine.
    PS648.C45M56 1997
    813'.0108334—dc21
        97-15467

            CIP

02   01   00   99   98   97
10   9   8   7   6   5   4   3   2   1

Contents

Introduction

No wonder we associate Christmas with miracles: We are celebrating God's coming to earth as a human baby. How could we keep our eyes closed to his light shining through history, to his light in the world around us today?

In this collection of twelve stories of the season, we see people of all ages and times experiencing miracles. By turns touching, humorous, inspiring, and even heart-changing, most of the stories recount miracles from everyday life. Proud hearts melt and receive forgiveness. Young and old people are freed to express their love— the Christmas season provides them with the "opportunity to speak kind feelin' right out." The miracle of giving enlarges the hearts of both givers and those who receive. And people in need come upon help just in time through chance encounters with strangers.

Parents and children, brothers and sisters, friends and strangers—these all come truly together around the holy child. And nature itself is joyously turned upside down in the celebration of Christ's birth and the hope-filled future his incarnation promises.

Perhaps the wonders recorded in these stories will help restore for you what often gets lost in modern Christmas celebrations—the understanding that God's presence in human history and in our own lives can bring miracles to us as well.

The Miracle of the Child

Star Over Bethlehem
Agatha Christie Mallowan

ary looked down at the baby in the manger. She was alone in the stable except for the animals. As she smiled down at the child her heart was full of pride and happiness.

Then suddenly she heard the rustling of wings and turning, she saw a great Angel standing in the doorway.

The Angel shone with the radiance of the morning sun, and the beauty of his face was so great that Mary's eyes were dazzled and she had to turn aside her head.

Then the Angel said (and his voice was like a golden trumpet): "Do not be afraid, Mary . . ."

And Mary answered in her sweet low voice: "I am not afraid, O Holy One of God, but the Light of your Countenance dazzles me."

The Angel said: "I have come to speak to you."

Mary said: "Speak on, Holy One. Let me hear the commands of the Lord God."

The Angel said: "I have come with no commands. But since you are specially dear to God, it is permitted that, with my aid, you should look into the future. . . ."

Then Mary looked down at the child and asked eagerly: "Into *his* future?"

Her face lit up with joyful anticipation.

"Yes," said the Angel gently. "Into *his* future . . . Give me your hand."

Mary stretched out her hand and took that of the Angel. It was like touching flame—yet flame that did not burn. She shrank back a little and the Angel said again: "Do not be afraid. I am immortal and you are mortal, but my touch shall not hurt you. . . ."

Then the Angel stretched out his great golden wing over the sleeping child and said: "Look into the future, Mother, and see your Son. . . ."

And Mary looked straight ahead of her and the stable walls melted and dissolved and she was looking into a Garden. It was night and there were stars overhead and a man was kneeling, praying.

Something stirred in Mary's heart, and her motherhood told her that it was her son who knelt there. She said thankfully to herself: "He has become a good man—a devout man—he prays to God." And then suddenly she caught her breath, for the man had raised his face and she saw the agony on it—the despair and the sorrow . . . and she knew that she was looking on greater anguish than any she had ever known or seen. For the man was utterly alone. He was praying to God, praying that this cup of anguish might be taken from him—and there was no answer to his prayer. God was absent and silent. . . .

And Mary cried out: "Why does not God answer him and give him comfort?"

And she heard the voice of the Angel say: "It is not God's purpose that he should have comfort."

Then Mary bowed her head meekly and said: "It is not for us to know the inscrutable purposes of God. But has this man—my son—has he no friends? No kindly human friends?"

The Angel rustled his wing and the picture dissolved into another part of the Garden and Mary saw some men lying asleep.

She said bitterly: "He needs them—my son needs them—and they do not care!"

The Angel said: "They are only fallible human creatures . . ."

Mary murmured to herself: "But he is a *good* man, my son. A good and upright man."

Then again the wing of the Angel rustled, and Mary saw a road winding up a hill, and three men on it carrying crosses, and a crowd behind them and some Roman soldiers.

The Angel said: "What do you see now?"

Mary said: "I see three criminals going to execution."

The left hand man turned his head and Mary saw a cruel crafty face, a low bestial type—and she drew back a little.

"Yes," she said, "they are criminals."

Then the man in the centre stumbled and nearly fell, and as he turned his face, Mary recognised him and she cried out sharply: "No, no, it cannot be that my son is a *criminal!*"

But the Angel rustled his wing and she saw the three crosses set up, and the figure hanging in agony on the centre one was the man she knew to be her son. His cracked lips parted and she heard the words that came from them: *"My God, my God, why hast thou forsaken me?"*

And Mary cried out: "No, no, it is not true! He cannot have done anything really wrong. There has been some dreadful mistake. It can happen sometimes. There has been some confusion of identity; he has been mistaken for someone else. He is suffering for someone else's crime."

But again the Angel rustled his wing and this time Mary was looking at the figure of the man she revered most on earth—the High Priest of her Church. He was a noble-looking man, and he stood up now and with solemn hands he tore and rent the garment he was wearing, and cried out in a loud voice: "This man has spoken Blasphemy!"

And Mary looked beyond him and saw the figure of the man who had spoken Blasphemy—and it was her son.

Then the pictures faded and there was only the mudbrick wall of the stable, and Mary was trembling and crying out brokenly: "I cannot believe it—I *cannot* believe it. We are a God-fearing straight-living family—all my family. Yes, and Joseph's family too. And we shall bring him up carefully to practise religion and to revere and honour the faith of his fathers. A son of ours could never be guilty of Blasphemy—I cannot believe it! All this that you have shown me cannot be true."

Then the Angel said: "Look at me, Mary."

And Mary looked at him and saw the radiance surrounding him and the beauty of his Face.

And the Angel said: "What I have shown you is Truth. For I am the Morning Angel, and the Light of the Morning is Truth. Do you believe now?"

And sorely against her will, Mary knew that what she had been shown was indeed Truth . . . and she could not disbelieve any more.

The tears raced down her cheeks and she bent over the child in the manger, her arms outspread as though to protect him. She cried out: "My child . . . my little helpless child . . . what can I do to save you? To spare you from what is to come? Not only from the sorrow and the pain, but from the evil that will blossom in your heart? Oh indeed it would have been better for you if you had never been born, or if you had died with your first breath. For then you would have gone back to God pure and unsoiled."

And the Angel said: "That is why I have come to you, Mary."

Mary said: "What do you mean?"

The Angel answered: "You have seen the future. It is in your power to say if your child shall live or die."

Then Mary bent her head, and amidst stifled sobs she murmured: "The Lord gave him to me . . . If the Lord now takes him away, then I see that it may indeed be mercy, and though it tears my flesh I submit to God's will."

But the Angel said softly: "It is not quite like that. God lays no command on you. The choice is *yours*. You have seen the future. Choose now if the child shall live or die."

Then Mary was silent for a little while. She was a woman who thought slowly. She looked once at the Angel for guidance, but the Angel gave her none. He was golden and beautiful and infinitely remote.

She thought of the pictures that had been shown her—of the agony in the garden, of the shameful death, of a man who, at the hour of death, was forsaken of God, and she heard again the dreadful word *Blasphemy*. . . .

And now, at this moment, the sleeping babe was pure and innocent and happy. . . .

But she did not decide at once, she went on thinking—going over and over again those pictures she had been shown. And in doing so a curious thing happened, for she remembered little things that she had not been aware of seeing at the time. She saw, for instance, the face of the man on the right-hand cross. . . . Not an evil face, only a weak one—and it was turned towards the centre cross and on it was an expression of love and trust and adoration. . . . And it came to Mary, with sudden wonder— "It was at *my son* he was looking like that . . ."

And suddenly, sharply and clearly, she saw her son's face as it had been when he looked down at his sleeping friends in the garden. There was sadness there, and pity and understanding and a great love . . . And she thought: "It is the face of a *good* man . . ." And she saw again the scene of accusation. But this time she looked, not at the splendid High Priest, but at the face of the accused man . . . and in his eyes was no consciousness of guilt. . . .

And Mary's face grew very troubled.

Then the Angel said: "Have you made your choice, Mary? Will you spare your son suffering and evildoing?"

And Mary said slowly: "It is not for me, an ignorant and simple woman, to understand the High Purposes of God. The Lord gave me my child. If the Lord takes him away, then that is His will. But since God has given him life, it is not for me to take that life away. For it may be that in my child's life there are things that I do not properly understand . . . It may be that I have seen only *part* of a picture, not the whole. My baby's life is his own, not mine, and I have no right to dispose of it."

"Think again," said the Angel. "Will you not lay your child in my arms and I will bear him back to God?"

"Take him in your arms if it is God's command," said Mary. "But *I* will not lay him there."

There was a great rustling of wings and a blaze of light and the Angel vanished.

Joseph came in a moment later and Mary told him of what had occurred. Joseph approved of what Mary had done. "You did right wife," he said. "And who knows, this may have been a lying Angel."

"No," said Mary. "He did not lie." She was sure of that with every instinct in her.

"I do not believe a word of it all," said Joseph stoutly. "We will bring our son up very carefully and give him good religious instruction, for it is education that counts. He shall work in the shop and go with us to the Synagogue on the Sabbath and keep all the Feasts and the Purifications."

Looking in the manger, he said: "See, our son is smiling . . ."

And indeed the boy was smiling and holding out tiny hands to his mother as though to say "Well Done."

But aloft in the vaults of blue, the Angel was quivering with pride and rage. "To think that I should fail with a foolish, ignorant woman! Well, there will come another chance. One day when *He* is weary and hungry and weak . . . Then I will take him up to the top of a mountain and show him the Kingdoms of this World of mine. I will offer him the Lordship of them all. He shall control Cities and Kings and Peoples . . . He shall have the Power of causing wars to cease and hunger and oppression to vanish. One gesture of worship to me and he shall be able to establish peace and plenty, contentment and good will—know himself to be a Supreme Power for Good. He can never withstand *that* temptation!"

And Lucifer, Son of the Morning, laughed aloud in ignorance and arrogance and flashed through the sky like a burning streak of fire down to the nethermost depths. . . .

In the East, three Watchers of the Heavens came to their Masters and said: "We have seen a Great Light in the Sky. It must be that some great Personage is born."

But whilst all muttered and exclaimed of Signs and Portents a very old Watcher murmured: "A Sign from God? God has no need of Signs and Wonders. It is more likely to be a Sign from Satan. It is in my mind that if God were to come amongst us, he would come very quietly. . . ."

But in the Stable there was much fun and good company. The ass brayed, and the horses neighed and the oxen lowed, and men and women crowded in to see the baby and passed him from one to the other, and he laughed and crowed and smiled at them all. "See," they cried. "He loves everybody! There never was such a Child. . . ."

The Child in the Midst

Patricia St. John

Margaret slithered off the stepladder with a bump, and her husband, stretched out in an armchair in front of the television with his eyes shut, came to with a start.

"What on earth are you doing?" he asked, rather irritably.

"Putting up the mistletoe," she replied, and felt guilty. It was absurd, at her age, to be scrambling up stepladders, clinging to the old ways. George, her husband, thought so too, and, besides, it made him uncomfortable. If she had such a hankering after mistletoe he supposed he ought to be doing it for her, but he was dead tired with weeks of working overtime. If only he could just stay slumped in his chair for his three days' Christmas leave; but he supposed he ought to make some effort. He looked round at the tree and the paper decorations, trying to affect an enthusiasm he did not feel.

"Looks fine!" he said, "but why mistletoe? I hope Angela's not bringing that friend of hers here; can't make head or tail of him; not my type!"

"Oh, Angela's spending Christmas evening over at his place," answered Margaret with studied carelessness. "She told me so this morning. And Jimmy's off to some party, too. But we shall all be

together for Christmas dinner, and after dinner we'll have the presents and the tree."

He looked at her anxiously. She was tired out, too, getting it all ready, and Jimmy and Angela would probably be so full of their own affairs that they would hardly notice it. Selfish little beggars, he thought angrily, why hadn't they helped her instead of dashing off to a Christmas Eve dance?

"Aren't they a bit old for a Christmas tree?" he said rather lamely.

"Yes," she answered, "but we must have one this year, because of Gustav. Children must have Christmas trees." She did not add how thankful she was for Gustav. A child in the house held everything together. Because of him she could keep up the old traditions just for one more year. She felt in her heart that they were all drifting apart, but the tree was a sort of anchor drawing them back to the days when they hung up their stocking at night and all stayed together. Perhaps through Gustav they could recapture something of that spirit, just for an hour or two at dinner time.

"Well, I hope he'll rise to the occasion," said George doubtfully. "Queer little soul, isn't he? I wish he'd rowdy about a bit—downright unnatural for a child to be so quiet."

"He's suffered a lot," said Margaret. "Life in a refugee camp must break a child's spirit. Mrs. Himmler isn't exactly cheerful either, but she's a very good worker."

"No, she's not exactly a ray of sunshine," added George. "I should think they have both gone through it. Has she told you any details?"

"No, she's kept herself to herself so far," said Margaret. "She's not too good at English, and, besides, we've been so busy getting ready for Christmas, there's been no time to talk."

She went out into the kitchen to put the finishing touches on the cake, wondering dully when they would eat it. She had hidden her disappointment when Jimmy and Angela had both told her they would be out for tea and supper, but now in the quiet kitchen where no one could see her Margaret sat down for a moment and buried her face in her hands. She was so desperately tired. She thought she would go to bed and hope there would be time in the morning to finish off. They always used to go to church on Christmas morning, but if the children weren't home until after midnight she would never drag them out of bed in time, and it would be cruel to ask George. He seemed worn out these days, but his bank balance was rising so she supposed it was worth it.

A child's toy lay on the floor—Gustav's. Strange how she clung to the thought of Gustav, and he such a plain, uninteresting child!

Christmas dinner went off quite well. George had roused himself for the occasion, and he was really making an effort. The children had appeared about half-past eleven, rested and dressed in their best. They were on cool terms with each other because of some disparaging remarks Jimmy had made about Angela's young man, but they were both affectionate and grateful towards their parents. To Margaret it seemed that perhaps the children wanted to give all they could in the short time they could spare. She noticed Angela glancing at her watch for the second time.

Well, she would not keep them long now. They would light the Christmas tree and open their presents, and then they could go. The curtains were drawn and Jimmy switched on the colored electric bulbs on the tree. Then he went to call the Himmlers.

They were waiting by the kitchen door dressed in their shabby best. Mrs. Himmler walked up the passage with shy dignity, unsure of what was expected of her, but Gustav had lost all his shyness. He ran ahead, his face bright with joyful anticipation. "Why," thought Margaret holding open the door, "he looks like a real child, instead of a careworn old man!"

"Good heavens," murmured George. "Wouldn't have recognised him."

Neither would any of the rest of them. Gustav's pale cheeks were red with excitement, and the colored lights were reflected in his starry eyes. He stood for a few moments transfixed, staring at the tree, and then ran forward searching eagerly behind the expensive presents piled in front.

What was he looking for? He turned from the gifts and slipped behind George who was standing in front of the fireplace. Whatever Gustav searched for wasn't there either. He came out and stood, hesitant, still searching the room with his big, dark eyes. But the

stars had gone out of the eyes, and his face wore an expression of perplexed disappointment. His mother, too, was looking round wistfully, shyly.

"What is it, Gustav?" asked Margaret gently. "Have you lost something, or are you looking for your present? You shall have it in a moment. Look, it's here with the others."

He stared up at her.

"The Child?" he queried in a puzzled voice. "You haf forgotten the Child?"

"The child?" repeated Angela. "Which child?"

Gustav's mother rose swiftly and drew him to her. She whispered something in his ear and turned to the family.

"Gustav do not understand," she explained apologetically. "In Germany we have a *Krippe,* and at Christmas we remember the Christ Child. But I tell him in England it is not the custom. Now he understand *gut.*"

Yes, he understood now. He leaned against his mother, once again the pale, patient child they had known before, embarrassed at his own mistake. Then, to cover up the awkward moment, Margaret handed him his parcel. He smiled and thanked her, but he did not open it. He preferred to do that alone with his mother, in the kitchen.

Everyone was pleased with the gifts. Jimmy and Angela had been wonderfully generous with their first earnings. They must have saved for quite some time to produce that warm, cherry colored dressing gown for their mother. Margaret felt oddly shaken by the gift. She also recognized that under her daughter's gaiety and charming clothes Angela was restless and nervous. She had never been to her boyfriend's home before; the coming afternoon was fraught with fate.

Jimmy and Angela had gone off to their respective engagements, full of thanks, but obviously in a hurry. George was back in his armchair, apparently fast asleep. Margaret would not have minded a rest herself, but she thought she ought to help Mrs. Himmler with all that mound of dishes. Angela might have given a hand, she thought rather irritably and then checked herself. Angela was in the throes of conflict and seemed to have no one to turn to. Only by the tiniest hints had Margaret divined that Angela's eyes were being opened to the type of boy she had chosen. Outwardly she still praised him up to the skies. It would be a bitter blow to her pride if she had to admit what he was really like.

"Why can't she tell me about it?" thought Margaret wretchedly as she dried the dishes. "I've failed her badly. She never tells me anything."

She stretched out her hand for another plate and suddenly became aware of Mrs. Himmler at the sink. Mrs. Himmler never told her anything either. They'd been in the kitchen together for ten minutes and never said a word. It was absurd.

"Where is Gustav?" asked Margaret.

Mrs. Himmler gave one of her rare smiles and pointed to the warm scullery off the kitchen where they kept the immersion heater and aired the clothes. The door was shut. A strange place for a child to play, thought Margaret. But Mrs. Himmler apparently knew what he was doing, and she seemed to be waiting for something.

Soon the door of the little scullery opened and Gustav's head came round it. He did not see Margaret at first, but she saw him and marveled. His eyes were glowing with mysterious joy, his lips parted in wonder, his cheeks poppy-bright. He beckoned to his mother who dried her hands on her apron.

"Pardon me, madam," she said, a little timidly. "Gustav, he make somesing . . . I go and see . . . soon I come back."

Margaret clasped her hands. Perhaps her longing showed in her face, for Mrs. Himmler, with one hand in Gustav's, turned back, hesitating.

"May I see too?" asked Margaret.

As an answer, Gustav slipped his other hand into hers and beamed at her. He drew both women through the door and knelt down. Mrs. Himmler and Margaret knelt too. For a few moments they just worshipped; then they smiled at each other.

What they saw was a little crèche, beautifully made for a child of seven. Gustav had worked on it out in the yard for days. He had expected a very elaborate one in the drawing room, like those he had seen in past years in the church, but he had wanted one alone with his mother as well. The crib was hollowed from a piece of wood, and the star, cut from a piece of gold paper, hung above it. He had collected straw from an old packing case for his cardboard stable with its painted starry windows. The figures were of clay and his mother had bought him a toy cow and two lambs. The whole was lighted with one red candle, and his own presents were carefully arranged in front, cradled in fir boughs.

"It is custom," said Mrs. Himmler, slightly apologetic. "In our country every year we make the *Krippe,* and our family we all come together round the Child. Gustav, he remember . . . we sing, and father read from the Bible."

"Can't we sing now?" asked Margaret. No one was shy any longer. Gustav and his mother sang a little German carol, and Margaret taught them "Away in a Manger." Gustav nestled up to her, utterly content, satiated with happy memories. The afternoon drew in, and the candle burned with a pure, clear light.

Suddenly Mrs. Himmler began reminiscing . . . the terrible struggle of the past years . . . the little daughter who had died because food was so scarce . . . her husband shot down, trying to get to the West . . . their own escape to relatives in England who had not really had room for them. "But God led us," finished Mrs. Himmler simply. "He led us to you. We are happy here. You are *gut.*"

They talked a long time. They forgot they were mistress and maid; they were just two women talking about their children, their hopes, their fears. "We all come together round the Child," Mrs. Himmler had said, and that had always been true. King and shepherd had knelt on common ground at Bethlehem.

It was quite late when Margaret remembered George's tea and jumped guiltily to her feet.

Angela decided to come in at the back door and slip up to bed unnoticed. She did not want to face her parents and answer their kind questions. Tomorrow, little by little, she would let them know that her relationship was now a thing of the past. Not tonight. They would want explanations and she could never explain. There had been no open row. She had just seen her boyfriend at home finally, in his natural setting of vulgarity and drink. She had noticed the way he treated his parents, and all her secret misgivings had become certainties. In the end Angela had slipped out unnoticed—he had not even escorted her home.

Her clean pajamas were in the airing cupboard. When she realized the light was broken in the scullery, she lit a candle and went into the small room to look for them. On the threshold of the scullery, however, Angela stopped transfixed. Then she sat down on the floor, just as Gustav had done, her candle beside her. She began to cry. Why should she cry here, she wondered? She did not know yet that the manger was the symbol of the Word become flesh . . . touched with the feeling of their infirmities . . . the trysting place for broken hearts. She would learn that later.

Margaret stepped into the kitchen to get George a good-night drink. Startled by the small white light visible through the crack of the scullery door, she thought, "Surely we did not leave the candle burning all this time?" She stepped across to check, and then she stopped just as her daughter had. A moment later she was sitting on the floor beside Angela, and in shy broken phrases Angela was telling her all about her burden.

"It's no good," Angela finished, with a sniff. "I'll just have to make a clean break. It was horrible, Mummy. I didn't know he was like that . . . he seemed quite decent."

She did not add how she had longed for the clean, dull atmosphere of home. Nor did she describe how dear her simple, exasperating, old-fashioned mother seemed to her at that moment.

Margaret, searching for something comforting to say, gazed at the rough little crib and she found Mrs. Himmler's words mixing with her thoughts—*We all came together round the Child . . . she hasn't talked like this to me for months . . . if only I can help her to find her feet again. . . .*

Then George appeared at the kitchen door. "Where are you?" he called rather anxiously. "I thought you were bringing a drink."

"We're here," called Angela, and began to laugh. *Poor old Daddy, we keep forgetting all about him!*

"I'll make a pot of tea, Mummy," she said rising, "and I'll bring

in some chairs for you and Daddy. We might as well stay here; it's so warm and cosy by candlelight."

"Good heavens!" George exclaimed. "Did Gustav make that? Best thing I've seen this Christmas!" He sat down, the tea cloths dangling above his head. Angela brought the tea. There was a carol service on television which George had forgotten to switch off and the strains reached them as they sipped their steaming cups.

> O, little town of Bethlehem,
> How still we see thee lie! . . .
> The hopes and fears of all the years
> Are met in thee tonight.

Plenty of fears, thought Margaret. *Fears for George's health, for Angela's future; fears that we are all drifting apart. Plenty of hope too. We came together round the Child. What fools we have been ever to leave Him out . . . we have to start again somehow.*

> How silently, how silently,
> The wondrous gift is given! . . .
> Where meek souls will receive him, still
> The dear Christ enters in.

Silently! What a contrast to the last few hours, thought Angela, *with the radio blaring out meaningless music and the screams of empty laughter. What is a meek soul?* she wondered. *Is it just someone needy and longing to start again? Could that include me? Poor little Gustav was right—We have forgotten the Child!*

> . . . Oh, come to us, abide with us,
> Our Lord Emmanuel.

I wish it could always be like this, thought George, closing his eyes again. "Abide with us" not just on Christmas, but this sense of peace come to stay. How tired he was! Striving day in and day out, too tired to enjoy what he had earned or even to know about his children's affairs. Why, they'd all lived in separate compartments lately.

Only tonight, at the feet of that forgotten Child, had they found any sort of unity.

Jimmy locked his new cycle in the garage and hurled himself into the kitchen, slamming the back door behind him. He was cold and cross. His machine had not made quite the impression he had hoped for—one of the other fellows had been given a brand new motorbike. Jimmy felt unhappy about being so late. Mum had obviously been very disappointed when he had gone out, and now to make matters worse they'd apparently all gone to bed. There was no light in the drawing room although, strangely enough, they had left the television on and a candle burning.

Jimmy charged into the scullery and stopped short in astonishment.

"Gosh!" he cried. "Have you all gone daft?"

"Yes," answered his father, laughing in a way they had not heard for weeks. "Come and have a cuppa, Jimmy."

"Rather," replied Jimmy, his spirits mounting, "and what about that cake? Isn't this just the moment?"

How daft we must look, thought Jimmy, chuckling into his tea, *all huddled here round Gustav's crib in the back scullery. Next year we must remember to give him all the room he wants under the tree. Next year Gustav's crib should dominate the scene.*

He glanced across at Angela who was curled up on the rug, leaning against her mother's knees. Gosh! what a pretty kid she was. He hadn't expected her home so soon, and she'd been crying too, so probably something had gone wrong with the boyfriend. It was high time she came to her senses, but he could have kicked himself for the way he had sneered at her friend the night before. What right had he to judge when he wasn't offering anything in the way of sympathy or protection? When he thought about it, was he doing anything more than wasting time with that crowd he called his own friends? Somehow by that quiet candlelight shining on the crib, one saw things more clearly.

"On earth Peace, good will toward men," proclaimed the reader at the carol service, and the cathedral organ took up the theme.

Across the soft white candle glow Jimmy smiled at his sister and she understood perfectly. She smiled back, and handed him his third slice of cake.

The Flight into Egypt

Selma Lagerlöf

Far away, in a desert in the East, there grew, many years ago, a palm that was very, very old, and very, very tall. No one passing through the desert could help stopping to look at it, for it was much higher than other palms, and people said of it that it would surely grow to be higher than the obelisks and pyramids.

This great palm, standing in its loneliness, and looking over the desert, one day saw something which caused its huge crown of leaves to wave to and fro with surprise on its slender stem. On the outskirts of the desert two lonely persons were wandering. They were still so far away that even a camel would have looked no larger than an ant at that distance, but they were assuredly human beings, two who were strangers to the desert—for the palm knew the people of the desert—a man and a woman, who had neither guide, nor beasts of burden, nor tent, nor water-bag.

"Verily," said the palm to itself, "these two have come hither to die."

The palm looked quickly around.

"I am surprised," it said, "that the lions have not already gone out to seize their prey. But I do not see a single one about. Nor do I see any of the robbers of the desert. But they are sure to come.

"There awaits them a sevenfold death," thought the palm. "The lions will devour them, the serpents will sting them, thirst will consume them, the sand-storm will bury them, the robbers will kill them, the burning sun will overcome them, fear will destroy them."

The palm tried to think of something else; the fate of these two made it sad. But in the immeasurable desert around it there was not a single thing that the palm had not known and gazed at for thousands of years. Nothing could attract its attention. It was again obliged to think of the two wanderers. "By the drought and the wind!" said the palm, invoking the two greatest enemies of life, "what is the woman carrying on her arm! I believe these mad people have a little child with them!"

The palm, which was long-sighted, as the aged generally are, saw aright. The woman carried in her arms a child that had laid its head on her breast and was sleeping.

"The child has not even enough clothes on," said the palm. "I see that the mother has lifted up her skirt and thrown it over it. She has taken it out of its bed in great haste and hurried away with it. Now I understand: these people are fugitives.

"But they are mad, all the same," continued the palm. "If they have not an angel to protect them, they should rather have let their enemies do their worst than have taken refuge in the desert. I can imagine how it has all happened. The man is at work, the child sleeps in its cradle, the woman has gone to fetch water. When she has gone a few steps from the door she sees the enemy approaching. She rushes in, seizes the child, calls to the husband that he shall follow her, and runs away. Since then they have continued their flight the whole day; they have assuredly not rested a single moment. Yes, so it has all happened; but I say all the same, if no angel protects them—

"They are in such fear that they do not feel either fatigue or other sufferings, but I read thirst in their eyes. I think I should know the face of a thirsty man."

And when the palm began to think about thirst a fit of trembling went through its high stem, and the innumerable fronds of its long leaves curled up as if held over a fire.

"If I were a man," it said, "I would never venture into the desert. He is truly brave who ventures here without having roots reaching down to the inexhaustible water-veins. There can be danger even for palms, even for such a palm as I. Could I advise them, I would beg them to return. Their enemies could never be as cruel to them as the desert. They think perhaps that it is easy to live in the desert. But I know that even I at times have had difficulty in keeping alive. I remember once in my youth when a whirlwind threw a whole mountain of sand over me, I was nearly choking. If I *could* die I should have died then."

The palm continued to think aloud, as lonely old people do.

"I hear a wonderful melodious murmur passing through my crown," it said; "all the fronds of my leaves must be moving. I do not know why the sight of these poor strangers moves me so. But this sorrowful woman is so beautiful! It reminds me of the most wonderful thing that ever happened to me."

And whilst its leaves continued their melodious rustle the palm remembered how once, long, long ago, a glorious human being had visited the oasis. It was the Queen of Sheba, accompanied by the wise King Solomon. The beautiful Queen was on her way back to her own country; the King had accompanied her part of the way, and now they were about to part. "In memory of this moment," said the Queen, "I now plant a date-kernel in the earth; and I ordain that from it shall grow a palm which shall live and grow until a King is born in Judæa greater than Solomon." And as she said this she placed the kernel in the ground, and her tears watered it.

"How can it be that I should just happen to think of this today?" said the palm. "Can it be possible that this woman is so beautiful that she reminds me of the most beautiful of all queens, of her at whose bidding I have lived and grown to this very day? I hear my leaves rustling stronger and stronger," said the palm, "and it sounds sorrowful, like a death-song. It is as if they prophesied that someone should soon pass away. It is well to know that it is not meant for me, inasmuch that I cannot die."

The palm thought that the death-song in its leaves must be for the two lonely wanderers. They themselves surely thought that their last hour was drawing near. One could read it in their faces when they walked past one of the skeletons of the camels that lay by the roadside. One saw it from the glances with which they watched a couple of vultures flying past. It could not be otherwise—they must perish.

They had now discovered the palm in the oasis, and hastened thither to find water. But when they at last reached it they sank down in despair, for the well was dried up. The woman, exhausted, laid down the child, and sat down crying by the side of the well. The man threw himself down by her side; he lay and beat the ground with his clenched hands. The palm heard them say to each other that they must die. It also understood from their conversation that King Herod had caused all children of two or three years of age to be killed from fear that the great expected King in Judæa had been born.

"It rustles stronger and stronger in my leaves," said the palm. "These poor fugitives have soon come to their last moment."

It also heard that they were afraid of the desert. The man said it would have been better to remain and fight the soldiers than to flee. He said that it would have been an easier death.

"God will surely help us," said the woman.

"We are all alone amongst serpents and beasts of prey," said the man. "We have no food and no water. How can God help us?"

He tore his clothes in despair and pressed his face against the earth. He was hopeless, like a man with a mortal wound in his heart.

The woman sat upright, with her hands folded upon her knees. But the glances she cast over the desert spoke of unutterable despair.

The palm heard the sorrowful rustling in its leaves grow still stronger. The woman had evidently heard it too, for she looked up to the crown of the tree, and in the same moment she involuntarily raised her arms.

"Dates, dates!" she cried.

There was such a longing in her voice that the old palm wished it had not been any higher than the gorse, and that its dates had been as easy to reach as the red berries of the hawthorn. It knew that its crown was full of clusters of dates, but how could man reach to such a dazzling height?

The man had already seen that, the dates being so high, it was impossible to reach them. He did not even lift his head. He told his wife that she must not wish for the impossible.

But the child, which had crawled about alone and was playing with sticks and straws, heard the mother's exclamation. The little one could probably not understand why his mother should not have everything she wished for. As soon as he heard the word *dates*, he began to look at the tree. He wondered and pondered how he should get the dates. There came almost wrinkles on his forehead under the fair locks. At last a smile passed over his face. Now he knew what he would do. He went to the palm, stroked it with his little hand, and said in his gentle, childish voice: "Bend down, palm. Bend down, palm."

But what was this, what could this be? The palm-leaves rustled, as if a hurricane rushed through them, and shudder upon shudder passed through the tall stem. And the palm felt that the little one was the stronger. It could not resist him.

And with its high stem it bowed down before the child, as men bow down before princes. In a mighty arch it lowered itself towards earth, and at last bowed so low that its great crown of trembling leaves swept the sand of the desert.

The child did not seem to be either frightened or surprised, but with a joyous exclamation it ran and plucked one cluster after another from the crown of the old palm.

When the child had gathered enough, and the tree was still lying on the earth, he again went to it, stroked it, and said in his gentlest voice: "Arise, palm, arise."

And the great tree raised itself silently and obediently on its stem, whilst the leaves played like harps.

"Now I know for whom they play the death-song," the old palm said to itself, when it again stood erect. "It is not for any of these strangers."

But the man and woman knelt down on their knees and praised God.

"Thou hast seen our fear and taken it from us. Thou art the

Mighty One, that bends the stem of the palm like a reed. Of whom should we be afraid when Thy strength protects us?"

Next time a caravan passed through the desert, one of the travellers saw that the crown of the great palm had withered.

"How can that have happened?" said the traveller. "Have we not heard that this palm should not die before it had seen a King greater than Solomon?"

"Perhaps it has seen Him," answered another wanderer of the desert.

The Miracle of a Gift

Alice's Christmas-Tree
Edward Everett Hale

1

Alice MacNeil had made the plan of this Christmas-tree, all by herself and for herself. She had a due estimate of those manufactured trees which hard-worked "Sabbath Schools" get up for rewards of merit for the children who have been regular, and at the last moment have saved attendance-tickets enough. Nor did Alice Mac-Neil sit in judgment on these. She had a due estimate of them. But for her Christmas-tree she had two plans not included in those more meritorious buddings and bourgeonings of the winter. First, she meant to get it up without any help from anybody. And, secondly, she meant that the boys and girls who had anything from it should be regular laners and by-way farers,—they were to have no tickets of respectability,—they were not in any way to buy their way in; but, for this once, those were to come in to a Christmas-tree who happened to be ragged and in the streets when the Christmas-tree was ready.

So Alice asked Mr. Williams, the minister, if she could have one of the rooms in the vestry when Christmas Eve came; and he, good saint, was only too glad to let her. He offered, gently, his assistance in sifting out the dirty boys and girls, intimating to Alice that there was dirt and dirt; and that, even in those lowest depths which she was plunging into, there were yet lower deeps which she might find it wise to shun. But here Alice told him frankly that she would rather try her experiment fairly through. Perhaps she was wrong, but she would like to see that she was wrong in her own way. Any way, on Christmas Eve, she wanted no distinctions.

That part of her plan went bravely forward.

Her main difficulty came on the other side,—that she had too many to help her. She was not able to carry out the first part of her plan, and make or buy all her presents herself. For everybody was pleased with this notion of a truly catholic or universal tree; and everybody wanted to help. Well, if anybody would send her a box of dominos, or a jack-knife, or an open-eye-shut-eye doll, who was Alice to say it should not go on the tree? And when Mrs. Hesperides sent round a box of Fayal oranges, who was Alice to say that the children should not have oranges? And when Mr. Gorham Parsons sent in well-nigh a barrel full of Hubbardston None-such apples, who was Alice to say they should not have apples? So the tree grew and grew, and bore more and more fruit, till it was clear that there would be more than eighty reliable presents on it, besides apples and oranges, almonds and raisins galore.

Now you see this was a very great enlargement of Alice's plan; and it brought her to grief, as you shall see. She had proposed a cosey little tree for fifteen or twenty children. Well, if she had held to that, she would have had no more than she and Lillie, and Mr. Williams, and Mr. Gilmore, and John Flagg, and I, could have managed easily, particularly if Mamma was there too. There would have been room enough in the chapel parlor; and it would have been, as I believe, just the pretty and cheerful Christmas jollity that Alice meant it should be. But when it came to eighty presents, and a company of eighty of the unwashed and unticketed, it became quite a different thing.

For now Alice began to fear that there would not be children enough in the highways and by-ways. So she started herself, as evening drew on, with George, the old faithful black major-domo, and she walked through the worst streets she knew anything of, of all those near the chapel; and, whenever she saw a brat particularly dirty, or a group of brats particularly forlorn, she sailed up gallantly, and, though she was frightened to death, she invited them to the tree. She gave little admittance cards, that said, "7 o'clock, Christmas Eve, 507 Livingstone Avenue," for fear the children would not remember. And she told Mr. Flagg that he and Mr. Gilmore might take some cards and walk out toward Williamsburg, and do the same thing, only they were to be sure that they asked the dirtiest and most forlorn children they saw. There was a friendly policeman with whom Alice had been brought into communication by the boys in her father's office, and he also was permitted to give notice of the tree. But he was also to be at the street door, armed with the strong arm of "The People of New York," and when the full quota of eighty had been admitted he was to admit no more.

Ah me! My poor Alice issued her cards only too freely. Better indeed, it seemed, had she held to her original plan; at least she thought so, and thinks so to this day. But I am not so certain. A hard time she had of it, however.

Quarter of seven found the dirty little packs in crowds around the door, with hundreds of others who thought they also were to find out what a "free lunch" was. The faithful officer Purdy was in attendance also; he passed in all who had the cards; he sent away legions, let me say, who had reason to dread him; but still there assembled a larger and larger throng about the door. Alice and Lillie, and the young gentlemen, and Mrs. MacNeil, were all at work up stairs, and the tree was a perfect beauty at last. They lighted up, and nothing could have been more lovely.

"Let them in!" said John Flagg rushing to the door, where expectant knocks had been heard already. "Let them in,—the smallest girls first!"

"Smallest girls," indeed! The door swung open, and a tide of boy and girl, girl and boy, boy big to hobble-de-hoy-dom, and girl big to young-woman-dom, came surging in, wildly screaming, scolding, pushing, and pulling. Omitting the profanity, these are the Christmas carols that fell on Alice's ear.

"Out o' that!" "Take that, then!" "Who are you?" "Hold your jaw!" "Can't you behave decent?" "You lie!" "Get out of my light!" "Oh, dear! you killed me!" "Who's killed?" "Golly! see there!" "I say, ma'am, give me that pair of skates!" "Shut up—" and so on, the howls being more and more impertinent, as the shepherds who had come to adore became more and more used to the position they were in.

Young Gilmore, who was willing to oblige Alice, but was not going to stand any nonsense, and would have willingly knocked the heads together of any five couples of this rebel rout, mounted on a corner of the railing, which, by Mr. Williams's prescience had been built around the tree, and addressed the riotous assembly.

They stopped to hear him, supposing he was to deliver the gifts, to which they had been summoned.

He told them pretty roundly that if they did not keep the peace, and stop crowding and yelling, they should all be turned out of doors; that they were to pass the little girls and boys forward first, and that nobody would have any thing to eat till this was done.

Some approach to obedience followed. A few little waifs were found, who in decency could be called *little* girls and boys. But, alas! As she looked down from her chair, Alice felt as if most of her guests looked like shameless, hulking big boys and big girls, only too well fitted to grapple with the world, and only too eager to accept its gifts without grappling. She and Lillie tried to forget this. They kissed a few little girls, and saw the faintest gleam of pleasure on one or two little faces. But there, also, the pleasure was almost extinct, in fear of the big boys and big girls howling around.

So the howling began again, as the distribution went forward. "Give me that jack-knife!" "I say, Mister, I'm as big as he is," "He had one before and hid it," "Be down, Tom Mulligan,—get off that fence or I'll hide you," "I don't want the book, give me them skates," "You sha'n't have the skates, I'll have 'em myself—" and so on. John Flagg finally knocked down Tom Mulligan, who had squeezed round behind the tree, in an effort to steal something, and had the satisfaction of sending him bellowing from the room, with his face covered with blood from his nose. Gilmore, meanwhile, was rapidly distributing an orange and an apple to each, which, while the oranges were sucked, gave a moment's quiet. Alice and the ladies, badly frightened, were stripping the tree as fast as they could, and at last announced that it was all clear, with almost as eager joy as half an hour before they had announced that it was all full. "There's a candy horn on top, give me that." "Give me that little apple." "Give me the old sheep." "Hoo! hurrah, for the old sheep!" This of a little lamb which had been placed as an appropriate ornament in front. Then began a howl about oranges. "I want another orange." "Bill's got some, and I've got none." "I say, Mister, give me an orange."

To which Mister replied, by opening the window, and speaking into the street,—"I say, Purdy, call four officers and come up and clear this room."

The room did not wait for the officers: it cleared itself very soon on this order, and was left a scene of wreck and dirt. Orange-peel trampled down on the floor; cake thrown down and mashed to mud, intermixed with that which had come in on boots, and the water which had been slobbered over from hasty mugs; the sugar plums which had fallen in scrambles, and little sprays of green too, trodden into the mass,—all made an aspect of filth like a market sidewalk. And poor Alice was half crying and half laughing; poor Lillie was wholly crying. Gilmore and Flagg were explaining to each other how gladly they would have thrashed the whole set.

The thought uppermost in Alice's mind was that she had been a clear, out and out fool! And that, probably, is the impression of the greater part of the readers of her story,—or would have been the impression of any one who only had her point of view.

2

Perhaps the reader is willing to take another point of view.

As the group stood there, talking over the riot as Mrs. MacNeil called it,—as John Flagg tried to make Alice laugh by bringing her a half-piece of frosted pound-cake, and proving to her that it had not been on the floor,—as she said, her eyes streaming with tears, "I tell you, John! I am a fool, and I know I am, and nobody but a fool would have started such a row,"—as all this happened, Patrick Crehore came back for his little sister's orange which he had wrapped in her handkerchief and left on one of the book-racks in the room. Patrick was alone now, and was therefore sheepish enough, and got himself and his orange out of the room as soon as he well could. But he was sharp enough to note the whole position, and keen enough to catch Alice's words as she spoke to Mr.

Flagg. Indeed, the general look of disappointment and chagrin in the room, and the contrast between this filthy ruin and the pretty elegance of half an hour ago, were distinct enough to be observed by a much more stupid boy than Patrick Crehore. He went down stairs and found Bridget waiting, and walked home with the little toddler, meditating rather more than was his wont on Alice's phrase, "I tell you, I am a fool." Meditating on it, he haled Bridget up five flights of stairs and broke in on the little room where a table spread with a plentiful supply of tea, baker's bread, butter, cheese, and cabbage, waited their return. Jerry Crehore, his father, sat smoking, and his mother was tidying up the room.

"And had ye a good time, me darling? And ye've brought home your orange, and a doll too, and mittens too. And what did you have, Pat?"

So Pat explained, almost sulkily, that he had a checker-board, and a set of checker-men, which he produced; but he put them by as if he hated the sight of them, and for a minute dropped the subject, while he helped little Biddy to cabbage. He ate something himself, drank some tea, and then delivered his rage with much unction, a little profanity, great incoherency,—but to his own relief.

"It's a mean thing it is, all of it," said he, "I'll be hanged but it is! I dunno who the lady is; but we've made her cry bad, I know that; and the boys acted like Nick. They knew that as well as I do. The man there had to knock one of the fellows down, bedad, and served him right, too. I say, the fellows fought, and hollared, and stole, and sure ye'd thought ye was driving pigs down the Eighth Avenue, and I was as bad as the worst of 'em. That's what the boys did when a lady asked 'em to Christmas."

"That was a mean thing to do," said Jerry, taking his pipe from his mouth for a longer speech than he had ever been known to make while smoking.

Mrs. Crehore stopped in her dish-wiping, sat down, and gave her opinion. She did not know what a Christmas-tree was, having never seed one nor heared of one. But she did know that those who went to see a lady should show manners and behave like jintleman, or not go at all. She expressed her conviction that Tom Mulligan was rightly served, and her regret that he had not two black eyes instead of one. She would have been glad, indeed, if certain Floyds, and Sullivans, and Flahertys with whose names of baptism she was better acquainted than I am, had shared a similar fate.

This oration, and the oracle of his father still more, appeased Pat somewhat; and when his supper was finished, after long silence, he said, "We'll give her a Christmas present. We will. Tom Mulligan and Bill Floyd and I will give it. The others sha'n't know. I know what we'll give her. I'll tell Bill Floyd that we made her cry."

3

After supper, accordingly, Pat Crehore repaired to certain rendezvous of the younger life of the neighborhood, known to him, in search of Bill Floyd. Bill was not at the first, nor at the second, there being indeed no rule or principle known to men or even to archangels by which Bill's presence at any particular spot at any particular time could be definitely stated. But Bill also, in his proud free-will, obeyed certain general laws; and accordingly Pat found him inspecting, as a volunteer officer of police, the hauling out and oiling of certain hose at the house of a neighboring hose company. "Come here, Bill; I got something to show you."

Bill had already carried home and put in safe keeping a copy of Routledge's "Robinson Crusoe," which had been given to him.

He left the hose inspection willingly, and hurried along with Pat, past many attractive groups, not even stopping where a brewer's horse had fallen on the ground, till Pat brought him in triumph to the gaudy window of a shoeshop, lighted up gayly and full of the wares by which even shoe-shops lure in customers for Christmas.

"See there!" said Pat, nearly breathless. And he pointed to the very centre of the display, a pair of slippers made from bronze-gilt kid, and displaying a hideous blue silk bow upon the gilding. For what class of dancers or of maskers these slippers may have been made, or by what canon of beauty, I know not. Only they were the centre of decoration in the shoe-shop window. Pat looked at them with admiration, as he had often done, and said again to Bill Floyd, "See there, ain't them handsome?"

"Golly!" said Bill, "I guess so."

"Bill, let's buy them little shoes, and give 'em to her."

"Give 'em to who?" said Bill, from whose mind the Christmas-tree had for the moment faded, under the rivalry of the hose company, the brewer's horse, and the shop window. "Give 'em to who?"

"Why, her, I don't know who she is. The gal that made the what-do-ye-call-it, the tree, you know, and give us the oranges, where old Purdy was. I say, Bill, it was a mean dirty shame to make such a row there, when we was bid to a party; and I want to make the gal a present, for I see her crying, Bill. Crying cos it was such a row." Again, I omit certain profane expressions which did not add any real energy to the declaration.

"They is handsome," said Bill, meditatingly. "Ain't the blue ones handsomest?"

"No," said Pat, who saw he had gained his lodgment, and that the carrying his point was now only a matter of time. "The gould ones is the ones for me. We'll give 'em to the gal for a Christmas present, you and I and Tom Mulligan."

Bill Floyd did not dissent, being indeed in the habit of going as he was led, as were most of the "rebel rout" with whom he had an hour ago been acting. He assented entirely to Pat's proposal. By "Christmas" both parties understood that the present was to be made before Twelfth Night, not necessarily on Christmas Day. Neither of them had a penny; but both of them knew, perfectly well, that whenever they chose to get a little money they could do so.

They soon solved their first question, as to the cost of the coveted slippers. True, they knew, of course, that they would be ejected from the decent shop if they went in to inquire. But, by lying in wait, they soon discovered Delia Sullivan, a decent-looking girl they knew, passing by, and having made her their confidant, so far that she was sure she was not fooled, they sent her in to inquire. The girl returned to announce, to the astonishment of all parties, that the shoes cost six dollars.

"Hew!" cried Pat, "six dollars for them are! I bought my mother's new over-shoes for one." But not the least did he 'bate of his de-

termination, and he and Bill Floyd went in search of Tom Mulligan.

Tom was found as easily as Bill. But it was not so easy to enlist him. Tom was in a regular corner liquor store with men who were sitting smoking, drinking, and telling dirty stories. Either of the other boys would have been whipped at home if he had been known to be seen sitting in this place, and the punishment would have been well bestowed. But Tom Mulligan had had nobody thrash him for many a day till John Flagg had struck out so smartly from the shoulder. Perhaps, had there been some thrashing as discriminating as Jerry Flaherty's, it had been better for Tom Mulligan. The boys found him easily enough, but, as I said, had some difficulty in getting him away. With many assurances, however, that they had something to tell him, and something to show him, they lured him from the shadow of the comfortable stove into the night.

Pat Crehore, who had more of the tact of oratory than he knew, then boldly told Tom Mulligan the story of the Christmas-tree, as it passed after Tom's ejection. Tom was sour at first, but soon warmed to the narrative, and even showed indignation at the behavior of boys who had seemed to carry themselves less obnoxiously than he did. All the boys agreed that but for certain others who had never been asked to come, and ought to be ashamed to be there with them as were, there would have been no row. They all agreed that on some suitable occasion unknown to me and to this story they would take vengeance on these Tidds and Sullivans. When Pat Crehore wound up his statement, by telling how he saw the ladies crying, and all the pretty room looking like a pig-sty, Tom Mulligan was as loud as he was in saying that it was all wrong, and that nobody but blackguards would have joined in it, in particular such blackguards as the Tidds and Sullivans above alluded to.

Then to Tom's sympathizing ear was confided the project of the gold shoes, as the slippers were always called, in this honorable company. And Tom completely approved. He even approved the price. He explained to the others that it would be mean to give to a lady any thing of less price. This was exactly the sum which recommended itself to his better judgment. And so the boys went home, agreeing to meet Christmas morning as a Committee of Ways and Means.

To the discussions of this committee I need not admit you. Many plans were proposed: one that they should serve through the holidays at certain ten-pin alleys, known to them; one that they should buy off Fogarty from his newspaper route for a few days. But the decision was, that Pat, the most decent in appearance, should dress up in a certain Sunday suit he had, and offer the services of himself, and two unknown friends of his, as extra cork-boys at Birnebaum's brewery, where Tom Mulligan reported they were working nights, that they might fill an extra order. This device succeeded. Pat and his friends were put on duty, for trial, on the night of the 26th; and, the foreman of the corking-room being satisfied, they retained their engagements till New Year's Eve, when they were paid three dollars each, and resigned their positions.

"Let's buy her three shoes!" said Bill, in enthusiasm at their success. But this proposal was rejected. Each of the other boys had a private plan; for an extra present to "her" by this time. The sacred six dollars was folded up in a bit of straw paper from the brewery, and the young gentlemen went home to make their toilets, a process they had had no chance to go through, on Christmas Eve. After this, there was really no difficulty about their going into the shoe-shop, and none about consummating the purchase,—to the utter astonishment of the dealer. The gold shoes were bought, rolled up in paper, and ready for delivery.

Bill Floyd had meanwhile learned, by inquiry at the chapel, where she lived, though there were doubts whether any of them knew her name. The others rejected his proposals that they should take street cars, and they boldly pushed afoot up to Clinton Avenue, and rang, not without terror, at the door.

Terror did not diminish when black George appeared, whose acquaintance they had made at the tree. But fortunately George did not recognize them in their apparel of elegance. When they asked for the "lady that gave the tree," he bade them wait a minute, and in less than a minute Alice came running out to meet them. To the boys' great delight, she was not crying now.

"If you please, ma'am," said Tom, who had been commissioned as spokesman,—"if you please, them's our Christmas present to you, ma'am. Them's gold shoes. And please, ma'am, we're very sorry there was such a row at the Christmas, ma'am. It was mean, ma'am. Good-by, ma'am."

Alice's eyes were opening wider and wider, nor at this moment did she understand. "Gold shoes," and "row at the Christmas," stuck by her, however; and she understood there was a present. So, of course, she said the right thing, by accident, and did the right thing, being a lady through and through.

"No, you must not go away. Come in, boys, come in. I did not know you, you know." As how should she. "Come in and sit down."

"Can't ye take off your hat?" said Tom, in an aside to Pat, who had neglected this reverence as he entered. And Tom was thus a little established in his own esteem.

And Alice opened the parcel, and had her presence of mind by this time; and, amazed as she was at the gold shoes, showed no amazement,—nay, even slipped off her own slipper, and showed that the gold shoe fitted, to the delight of Tom, who was trying to explain that the man would change them if they were too small. She found an apple for each boy, thanked and praised each one separately; and the interview would have been perfect, had she not innocently asked Tom what was the matter with his eye. Tom's eye! Why, it was the black eye John Flagg gave him. I am sorry to say Bill Floyd sniggered; but Pat came to the front this time, and said "a man hurt him." Then Alice produced some mittens, which had been left, and asked whose those were. But the boys did not know.

"I say, fellars, I'm going down to the writing-school, at the Union," said Pat, when they got into the street, all of them being in the mood that conceals emotion. "I say, let's all go."

To this they agreed.

"I say, I went there last week Monday, with Meg McManus. I say, fellars, it's real good fun."

The other fellows, having on the unfamiliar best rig, were well aware that they must not descend to their familiar haunts, and all consented.

To the amazement of the teacher, these three hulking boys allied themselves to the side of order, took their places as they were bidden, turned the public opinion of the class, and made the Botany Bay of the school to be its quietest class that night.

To his amazement the same result followed the next night. And to his greater amazement, the next.

To Alice's amazement, she received on Twelfth Night a gilt valentine envelope, within which, on heavily ruled paper, were announced these truths:—

Marm,—The mitins wur Nora Killpatrick's. She lives inn Water street place behind the Lager Brewery.

Yours to command,

William Floyd.
Thomas Mulligan.
Patrick Crehore.

The names which they could copy from signs were correctly spelled.

To Pat's amazement, Tom Mulligan held on at the writing-school all winter. When it ended, he wrote the best hand of any of them.

To my amazement, one evening when I looked in at Longman's, two years to a day after Alice's tree, a bright black-eyed young man, who had tied up for me the copy of Masson's "Milton," which I had given myself for a Christmas present, said: "You don't remember me." I owned innocence.

"My name is Mulligan—Thomas Mulligan. Would you thank Mr. John Flagg, if you meet him, for a Christmas present he gave me two years ago, at Miss Alice MacNeil's Christmas-tree. It was the best present I ever had, and the only one I ever deserved."

And I said I would do so.

I told Alice afterward never to think she was going to catch all the fish there were in any school. I told her to whiten the water with ground-bait enough for all, and to thank God if her heavenly fishing were skillful enough to save one.

Teacher Jensen

Karin Michaelis

If the school children had cared to look about them while they were playing hide-and-seek during recess, they would have seen the sharp tower of a mighty building piercing the air beyond a distant clump of trees. Unless you knew better, you would have believed that it was a castle where knights and beautiful ladies ate game off golden plates and on Sundays regaled themselves with macaroons. But the school children did know better. They knew, forgot, and remembered again, that it was a prison standing near them, where prisoners lived, each in his own cell, never seeing each other except at church, where black masks disguised their faces. They knew and forgot and remembered again.

Lauritz Thomsen belonged there. Not that he had done anything to be ashamed of—God forbid! But his father was the cook for the prison, and Lauritz knew what the prisoners got to eat—and what they did not get. He lived, so to speak, in prison, but apart from these men with the black masks. He was so accustomed to taking the short cut across the fields to the high red wall and walking through the entrance portal, which was immediately closed and bolted after him, that it all seemed like nothing extraordinary. He could see it in no other light. But if his schoolmates began to ask him questions he would hold his peace and blush to the roots of his hair.

His mother worried and grieved about the prison, and sought as best she could to forget what was going on. Filling her windows with flowers, she tried to silence her unpleasant thoughts about the poor creatures breathing the deathly cellar air behind those iron bars. She laid by penny upon penny in the hope of saving enough to buy a little country inn, or any kind of establishment far away from the Living Cemetery, as the prison was called. During her dreams she cried aloud, waking her children, for she always saw people with black masks on their faces swarming behind walls and windows and threatening to kill her. Evil dreams arise from evil thoughts, it is said, but Frau Thomsen could have no evil thoughts. She had only once in her life gone through the prison. It still froze her with terror to think of it, and she could not understand how her husband could sing and enjoy himself at the end of his day's work. Nor could she comprehend how he could speak of the prisoners as if they were friends or comrades. When he began to carry on in this way, she would leave the room and not come back until he had promised to talk about something else.

Children are children. They can accustom themselves to wading in a river where crocodiles sleep, or to playing in a jungle where snakes hang from the trees. Children become accustomed to living near a prison just as they get used to a father who drinks or a mother who scolds. They think of it, forget it, and remember it again. Thoughts glide across their minds like shadows; for a moment everything seems dark, and suddenly the sun shines once more.

Whenever a prisoner escaped, the school children were thrown into a great commotion. They followed the pursuit from afar, listening to the shots, the alarm signals, the whistles. They leaned out of windows and saw the prison wardens rushing in all directions, on foot, and on horseback. Nothing was so exciting as a man hunt, either over winter snow or over green summer fields. When the fugitive was taken, peace descended upon all their souls. Now the only question was what punishment would be meted out to the victim, and all eyes were turned toward Lauritz. But Lauritz said nothing. He was ashamed without quite knowing why.

Prison and prisoners would be forgotten save when a boy or girl at play would suddenly gape at the high towers to the east, jutting up there above the forest.

The children had a new teacher. He was called Teacher Jensen—nothing more. If he had a Christian name, he was never called by it. Just Teacher Jensen. And Teacher Jensen was little and frail, and Teacher Jensen's voice was as little and frail as he. But there was a wonderful quality in his voice, like a violin that makes a much louder noise than anyone would believe possible. The children did not sleep in his classes. They were not even drowsy. In his classes they forgot to write notes to each other or secretly to eat bread and butter behind their desks. They only listened and asked questions. Teacher Jensen had an answer for everything. They could ask Teacher Jensen all kinds of questions. But sometimes he would shake his head and say: "I seem to have forgotten it. Let me think a minute." Or worse yet: "I don't know. I never knew it. But I will look it up. It is to be found in some book, or a friend will tell me the answer." The children found that there was something splendid about having a teacher of whom you could ask all kinds of questions and who sometimes did not know the answer offhand.

Teacher Jensen talked about new things and old, and his speech was not like pepper shaken from a pepper pot. Even while the children were playing in the fields, they would remember what he had said. Yes, it remained fast in their minds.

One day Teacher Jensen said that murder was by no means the worst thing a man could do, and that it was much worse to think or say or do evil to another human being, or to make a defenseless animal suffer. And the children were full of wonder. It seemed that a new door had been opened to them, and each passed through it, one after another. Yes, it was true, what he said. They understood his meaning clearly, but they cast their eyes down, for all of them knew they had often done what was much worse than murder. Perhaps they would do it again, but not willingly, never willingly. Yet there was another thing worse than murder, and that was to act without using your will.

One day Teacher Jensen brought with him a sick, whining little cat which he had found on his way to school. He had put it under his cloak to keep it warm, and he stroked its back and its sharp little head. It was an ugly, gray, dirty cat. Teacher Jensen did not tell the children what he was going to do with it, but simply sat with the cat in his lap and rubbed his cheek against its head. To the children this poor little sick gray cat was the whole world. They took a silent vow that they would cure it. Through Teacher Jensen's little gray cat they had peered deep into the soul of an animal, and what they saw was more beautiful and more pure than a human soul.

Teacher Jensen often went on Sunday excursions with the children. Whoever wanted to could come, and all of them wanted to. It so happened that one Sunday morning in the autumn they were walking among falling leaves, and the earth clung to their shoes in little lumps. It had been raining, and was likely to rain again. Traversing a bit of open country, they soon entered the big forest in the distance. Ahead of them was the "castle" that was a prison. Lauritz ran in to get a scarf. Teacher Jensen saw him and drew his hand over his eyes, and as he cast down his eyes it was clear that he had been crying; but no one asked anything, no one spoke. They arrived at a vast grove of fir trees standing in long rows, with their evergreen branches above and their yellow trunks below. Teacher Jensen explained that such a forest could grow from a mere handful of tiny grains. The children knew this perfectly well; yet it sounded quite new. They suddenly understood that trees lived, breathed, and thought, that they strove for the light as poor people strive for bread.

"Now let's begin the game," said Teacher Jensen. "Let's imagine that this forest of fir trees is a prison, and that we are all prisoners, each in his own cell. Let us do this for one hour. I am holding a watch in my hand. During that hour let no one speak, for we are prisoners, and speech is forbidden."

This was a new game, a peculiar game. The rain had stopped some time ago, but drops were still falling from the high trees. The children stood, each under his own tree, and felt the water dripping and dripping on cheeks and hands. The children stood with the water dripping off them, laughing and shouting to each other side by side cell by cell. Slowly the laughter died and their faces became serious. All eyes were directed toward Teacher Jensen, who stood with the watch in his hand. He seemed to see nobody, and did not announce when the hour should begin.

The children felt as if they ought to hold their breath, for surely something important and serious was afoot. It was not like the times when they had gone out with other teachers, when hatred and pride cropped up as soon as the school door was closed. This was serious, and each breath was like a bucketful of water from a deep, deep well. Was time standing still? Had not many hours already passed? Were they really prisoners after all? They did not crawl away, though there was nothing to stop them. Teacher Jensen did not look around him at all, yet as soon as any of the children thought of creeping away they could not help remembering what happened when a prisoner escaped and they heard the shots ring out, the alarm bells clang, the whistles blow, and saw the wardens riding off in all directions hunting the fugitive. Their feet would not obey them—they were bound fast by Teacher Jensen's word; the outstretched hand with the watch held them in their places. Yes, they were prisoners, each in his own cell, and darkness settled and a gentle mist descended, veil upon veil.

Was this what it was like being a prisoner?

The hour was up.

Everyone sighed with relief, yet they all stood quiet for a moment, as if they could not really believe that they had regained their freedom. Then they sprang up and clustered around Teacher Jensen, asking him questions. It was growing dark, and he put his watch in his pocket, saying: "It is just as hard to be a prison watchman as to be a prisoner."

The children had never thought of this before, and after a long pause Teacher Jensen added: "The lot of the prison warden is the hardest of all, for he can do nothing for the prisoners; and in his heart he wants to help them all he can, yet they are not able to read his thoughts."

And after another pause he said: "I knew a man who spent seventeen years in prison and then died there."

When Lauritz reached home his mother was sitting at the piano playing and singing. The smell of freshly baked cake filled the room. On the table stood a glass bowl of apples. Lauritz's father sat on a chair smoking his pipe. Without knowing just what he said or why he said it, Lauritz went up to the piano and whispered in his mother's ear: "When I am a big man I shall be a prison warden."

"What did you say," she cried. "A prison warden, Lauritz? In there with those people? Never!"

Lauritz repeated: "When I am a big man I shall be a prison warden."

And then something happened that was never explained. Who had the idea first no one knew. Perhaps it entered all those little heads at the same time, in that hour when they were standing, each a prisoner under his own tree, each in his own cell—just in a single hour.

When Teacher Jensen was told about the plan, he only nodded as if he had known about it long ago. But when they begged him to talk to the prison inspector, since their scheme was contrary to all regulations, he shook his head, saying: "It is your idea. You must carry it out. It is up to you, if you believe in yourselves, to stand fast by your beliefs."

That was two months before Christmas, and all the school children, big and little, boys and girls, were there. Money was the first necessity, and it had to be collected in modest amounts and earned in an honorable way. Teacher Jensen said that if the gift was not honest no good came of it. The children all saved the money that they would ordinarily have spent on sweets and on stamps for their albums. They went on little errands, chopped wood, carried water, and scrubbed milk cans, wooden buckets, and copper tubs. The money was put into a big earthenware pig that Teacher Jensen had put in the wardrobe at school. No one knew who gave the most or who gave the least.

Lauritz announced that, including the seventeen sick people, there were three hundred and ten prisoners in the jail.

In the middle of December the pig was broken and the money was counted over and over, but it did not amount to much. Then a little fellow came with his little private savings bank, and a girl with a little earthen receptacle in which she kept her spare pennies. That started them off. Many little hoardings destined for Christmas presents were emptied into the great common fund at school. See how it grew! Shiny paper was now brought, and flags and walnuts.

Every day the whole school stayed until supper time cutting out and pasting. The little girls made white and red roses. They wove baskets, gilded walnuts, pasted flags on little sticks, and cut out cardboard stars, painting them gold and silver. The little ones made, out of clay, birds' nests with eggs in them, and little horses and cows that they covered with bright colors so they looked like real live animals. The boys cut out photographs and made little boxes. With jig saws they fashioned napkin rings and paper weights.

Christmas trees were bought—three hundred and ten real fir trees, for which the gardener charged only twenty-five pfennigs apiece.

Teacher Jensen emptied his purse on the desk. It had once been black, but it had long since turned brown, and was full of cracks. "That belonged to the man who spent seventeen years in prison," he announced. "He had it there with him. He kept it there for seventeen long years."

No one asked who the man was, but the money had to be counted over many times, for the children's eyes were moist and they had to keep wiping the tears away.

On the Sunday before Christmas the children went with Teacher Jensen to the local store and bought a lot of tobacco and chocolate, almonds and raisins, playing cards and brightly colored handkerchiefs, and writing paper. And they got a lot of old Christmas books too, which were given to them free because they were at the bottom of the pile and were out of date.

The parents of the children had to contribute whether they wanted to or not, and bags full of cookies and nuts, playing cards and books, came out of each house.

Lauritz's father had spoken in all secrecy to the prison chaplain, who went as a representative to the inspector. But the inspector hemmed and hawed saying: "That goes against all regulations. It's impossible. It can't be allowed on any ground whatever." The chaplain was to have told this to Lauritz's father, and Lauritz was to have brought the news to the children that the plan had to be abandoned. But the chaplain said nothing to Lauritz's father, and the children did not know that it was impossible and could never be allowed.

All the parents, no matter how much they had to do, made a

point of going into the schoolhouse the day before Christmas and seeing the three hundred little sparkling Christmas trees, each laden with joy, each with its star on the top, each with its white and red roses, white and red flags, and white and red candles, each decorated with tinsel and hung with gifts. To every tree a little letter was fastened, written by a boy or a girl. What was in this letter only the writer and perhaps Teacher Jensen knew—for Teacher Jensen had to help the little ones who only knew how to print numbers and capital letters.

The church bells rang over the town and called the faithful to God's worship. The prison bells rang out over the prison and called the prisoners to the prison church. Before the school was drawn up a row of wagons which had been laden with the little Christmas trees. Each child then took his tree under his arm and set out, following the wagons, singing as he went. It was a Christmas party without snow, but a Christmas party just the same.

Stopping before the prison, they rang the bell, and asked to speak to the inspector. He came out, and the moment he appeared, Teacher Jensen and all the children began to sing: *"O du fröhliche, o du selige, gnadenbringende Weihnachtszeit. . . ."*

The inspector shook his head sadly and raised his hands in the air. It was impossible, absolutely impossible—he had said so. But the children kept right on singing, and seemed not to hear him. As the inspector afterward said, when the director of all the prisons in that district demanded an explanation: "A man is only human, and had you been in my place, Mr. Director, you would have done as I did, even if it had cost you your position."

Thus it came to pass that this one time Christmas was celebrated in each cell of the big prison—a good, happy, cheerful Christmas. When the prisoners came back from the worship of God with their black masks on their faces they found a Christmas tree in every cell, and the cell doors stood open until the candles burned out, and the prisoners received permission to go freely from cell to cell all through the corridor to look at each other's Christmas trees and gifts—to look at them and to compare them. But each prisoner thought that his little tree and his present were the most beautiful and the best of all.

When the last light had burned out, the doors were closed, and far into the night the prisoners sang the Christmas carols of their childhood, free from distress, grief, and all spitefulness.

And as the last light flickered out behind the high walls the thin figure of a man with his coat collar up over his ears and his hat pulled over his face crept along the prison wall. Through the night air he heard the voices singing, *"Stille Nacht, heilige Nacht."*

Clasping his hands tightly together and raising them aloft into the darkness, he cried: "I thank thee, father. Thy guilt has been atoned for ten times over."

The Secret of the Gifts

Paul Flucke

The story has been told for centuries now. The story of Gaspar, Melchior and Balthasar, and the gifts they brought to the newborn king. And of how they saw the star and followed it for weeks across mountain and valley and desert. In stately procession on their swaying beasts, they came and placed their treasures at the feet of the infant Savior.

And what were their gifts? Ah, you say, everyone knows that. They brought gold, frankincense and myrrh. So, since the earliest days, the story has been told.

But there you are wrong. The story is incomplete. You see, the story was told by those who had seen the wise men on their journey. And by those who stood by in wonderment as the wise men dismounted from their weary camels and strode to the door of the rude stable. They watched as the wise men held their jeweled caskets high before them. That much the world saw. And so the story has been told.

But that is not the whole story. And if you listen very carefully and very quietly, you shall hear the rest of it. You shall hear what happened when the wise men entered the stable. And you shall learn the secret of the gifts.

Gaspar

The first of the three visitors to approach the stable was Gaspar. His cloak was of the finest velvet, trimmed with flawless fur. At his waist and throat were clusters of gems, for Gaspar was a wealthy man.

Those who watched saw only that he paused at the stable door. "He prays," they whispered to one another as they saw Gaspar's lips move. But they were mistaken. They could not see that it was the Angel Gabriel, guarding the holy place, before whom Gaspar stopped.

"And who are you?" Gabriel asked in a voice that was firm but not unkind.

"I am Gaspar, and I come to worship the king," he replied.

"All who enter here must bring a gift," said Gabriel. "Have you a gift?"

"Indeed I have," said Gaspar, and he held aloft a finely wrought box. It was small, yet so heavy that his arms could hardly raise it. "I have brought bars of the purest gold."

"Your gift," said Gabriel somberly, "must be the essence of yourself. It must be something precious to your soul."

"Such have I brought," answered Gaspar confidently, the hint of a smile upon his lips.

"So shall it be," said Gabriel. And he too smiled as he held the door for Gaspar to enter.

And there, before the rough board wall of the stable, lay the king he had traveled so far to see. The light of the lamp fell across the tiny face and glinted back from the dark, bright eyes. In the shadows sat the parents, motionless and silent. And beyond them, Gaspar sensed the presence of the sheep and oxen who stood their reverent watch.

Gaspar advanced a step and then another. He was just about to kneel and lay his gold before the child when he stopped and stood erect. There in his outstretched hands lay not gold but a hammer. Its scarred and blackened head was larger than a man's fist. And its handle was of sinewy wood as long as a man's forearm.

"But, but—" Gaspar stammered as he stared, dumbfounded, at the heavy tool. And then softly, from behind him, he heard the voice of Gabriel.

"So shall it be, and so it is," said the angel. "You have brought the essence of yourself."

Gaspar turned indignantly. "A hammer? What foul magic is this?"

"None but the magic of truth," replied Gabriel. "What you hold in your hands is the hammer of your greed. You have used it to pound wealth from those who labor so that you may live in luxury. You have used it to build a mansion for yourself while others dwell in hovels. You have raised it against friends and made them into enemies—and against enemies to destroy them."

And suddenly Gaspar knew the truth. Bowed with shame, he turned toward the door to leave.

But Gabriel blocked his way. "No, no," he said, "you have not offered your gift."

"Give *this?*" Gaspar blurted in horror, looking at the hammer. "I cannot give this to a king!"

"But you must," Gabriel replied. "That is why you came. And you cannot take it back with you. It is too heavy. You have carried it for many years, and even now your arms ache with its weight. You must leave it here, or it will destroy you."

And once again, Gaspar knew that the angel spoke the truth. But still he protested. "The hammer is too heavy," he said. "Why, the child cannot lift it."

"He is the only one who can," replied the angel.

"But it is dangerous. He might bruise his hands or feet."

"That worry," said Gabriel, "you must leave to heaven. The hammer shall find its place."

Slowly Gaspar turned to where the Christ child lay. And slowly he placed the ugly hammer at the baby's feet. Then he rose and turned to the door, pausing only for an instant to look back at the tiny Savior before he rushed outside.

The waiting world saw only the smile that wreathed Gaspar's face as he emerged from the stable. His hands were raised, as though the wings of angels graced his fingers. That much the world saw, and so the story is told.

Melchior

Next to step to the door of the stable was Melchior, the learned Melchior. He was not so resplendent as Gaspar for he wore the darker robes of the scholar. But the length of his beard and the furrows in his brow bespoke one who had lived long with the wisdom of the ages. A hush fell over the onlookers as he too paused before the door. But only Melchior could see the angel who stood guard. Only Melchior could hear him speak.

What have you brought?" asked Gabriel.

And Melchior replied, "I bring frankincense, the fragrance of hidden lands and bygone days."

"Your gift," cautioned Gabriel as he had done before, "must be something precious to your soul."

"Of course it is," retorted Melchior.

"Then enter, and we shall see." And Gabriel opened the door.

Melchior stood breathless before the scene within. In all his many years of searching for elusive Truth, he had never sensed such a presence as this. He knelt reverently. And from beneath his robe he withdrew the silver flask of precious ointment.

But then he drew back and stared. The vessel in his hand was not silver at all. It was common clay, rough and stained as might be found in the humblest cupboard. Aghast, he pulled the stopper from its mouth and sniffed the contents. Then he leapt to his feet only to face the angel at the door.

"I have been tricked," he said, spitting the words with fury. "This is not the frankincense I brought!"

"What is it, then?" asked Gabriel.

"It is vinegar!" Melchior snarled as though it were a curse.

"So shall it be, and so it is," said Gabriel. "You have brought what you are made of."

"You are an angel of fools," Melchior snorted.

But Gabriel went on. "You bring the bitterness of your heart, the soured wine of a life turned grim with jealousy and hate. You have carried within you too long the memory of old hurts. You have hoarded your resentments and breathed on sparks of anger until they have become as embers smoldering within you. You have sought for knowledge. But you have filled your life with poison."

As he heard these words, Melchior's shoulders drooped. He turned his face away from Gabriel and fumbled with his robe, as though to hide the earthen jar. Silently he sidled toward the door.

Gabriel smiled gently and placed his hand on Melchior's arm. "Wait," he said. "You must leave your gift."

Melchior sighed with a pain that came from deep within him. "How I wish I could! How long have I yearned to empty my soul of its bitterness. You have spoken the truth, my friend. But I cannot leave it here! Not here, at the feet of love and innocence."

"But you can," said Gabriel. "And you must, if you would be clean. This is the only place you *can* leave it."

"But this is vile and bitter stuff," Melchior protested. "What if the child should touch it to his lips?"

"You must leave that worry to heaven," Gabriel replied. "There is a use even for vinegar."

So Melchior placed his gift before the Savior. And they say that when he came out of the stable, his eyes shone with the clearest light of heaven's truth. His skin was as smooth as a youth's as he lifted his face to gaze on horizons he had never seen before. And in that, at least, the story is correct.

Balthasar

There was yet one more visitor to make his offering. He strode forward now, his back as straight as a tree, shoulders firm as an oaken beam. He walked as one born to command. This was Balthasar, leader of many legions, scourge of walled cities. Before him, as he grasped it by its handle of polished ebony, he carried a brass-bound box.

A murmur ran through those who watched as they saw him hesitate before the door. "Look," they whispered, "even the great Balthasar does obeisance before the king who waits within."

But we know that it was Gabriel who caused the warrior to pause. And we know too the question that he put.

"Have you a gift?"

"Of course," answered Balthasar. "I bring a gift of myrrh, the most precious booty of my boldest conquest. Many have fought and died for centuries for such as this. It is the essence of the rarest herb."

"But is it the essence of yourself?" asked Gabriel.

"It is," replied the general.

"Then come," said the angel, "and we shall see."

Even the fearless Balthasar was not prepared for the wave of awe that struck him as he entered the holy place of the Christ child. He felt a weakness in his knees such as he had never known before. Closing his eyes, he knelt and shuffled forward through the straw in reverence. Then, bowing until his face was near the ground, he slowly released his grip upon the handle of the box and raised his head and opened his eyes.

What lay before him at the baby's feet was his own spear. Its smooth round staff still glistened where the sweat of his palms had moistened it. And the razor edges of its steely tip caught the flickering light of the lamp.

"It cannot be!" Balthasar whispered hoarsely. "Some enemy has cast a spell!"

"That is more true than you know," said Gabriel softly from behind him. "A thousand enemies have cast their spell on you and turned your soul into a spear."

"You speak in riddles," cried Balthasar, turning to face the angel. "I'll teach you not to jest at a time like this." And he raised his fist as if to strike.

Gabriel did not flinch as he continued: "Living only to conquer, you have been conquered. Each battle you win leads you only to another with a foe yet more formidable."

"Do you think I *like* to kill?" demanded Balthasar. "You angels know nothing of this world. I am the defender of my people. Were it not for my spear leading them in battle, we should have been destroyed long ago. Why, even now, the enemy is massing to invade us. As soon as I leave this holy place, I must raise more armies. I must buy more spears to arm them and—"

"More," Gabriel interrupted quietly, "than what?"

"Why, more than we have now. More than our enemies have."

"And what will they do then?" asked the angel softly. "Will your enemies too need more?"

Balthasar heard the angel's words, and they seemed to echo in the deepest places of his soul as though vaguely familiar. Was the question one that he had sometime asked himself? Was it that faintest flicker of doubt, quickly stifled by one who did not dare to doubt?

For a moment, Balthasar hesitated. Then, taking control of himself, he reached down and grasped his spear—and turned toward the door.

"I cannot leave this here," he said. "My people need it. We cannot afford to give it up."

"Are you sure," asked Gabriel, "that you can afford to *keep* it?"

"But our enemies will destroy us if we drop our spears," Balthasar said impatiently. "We cannot take that risk."

"Yes, it is a *risk*," Gabriel replied slowly. "But your way is a *certainty*—a certainty of spears."

Once again, Balthasar hesitated. And once again, the sweat of his palm moistened the smooth shaft of the spear. But now the beads stood out on his forehead as well, as the force of Gabriel's words did battle with centuries of warrior instinct.

A long moment passed. Finally Balthasar loosed his grip, and the spear drooped toward the floor. But as he looked at the child at his feet, he whispered anxiously to Gabriel, "But here? Is it safe to leave it here?"

The angel released a long-held breath as he whispered back, "This is the only safe place to leave it."

"But he is a child, and the spear is sharp. It could pierce his flesh."

"That fear you must leave to heaven," Gabriel replied.

And they say that Balthasar went calmly from the stable, his arms hanging gently at his sides. They say that he walked first to Gaspar and Melchior, where they waited, and embraced them as brothers. Then, turning to the others who watched, he went first to one and then to the next, enfolding each in his outstretched arms as one greeting beloved friends whom he has not seen for a very long time.

That, at least, is how the story has always been told. And it is true, as far as it goes. But you have listened well, and now you know the whole of it.

Now you too may kneel before the Christ child to leave at his feet those unseen, secret things that may be left nowhere else but there. And having visited the holy place, you too, like those three visitors of old, may go on your way made new.

But what of their gifts, you ask? What of the hammer and the vinegar and the spear? Well, there is another story about them and how they were seen once more, years later, in fact, on a lonely hill outside of Jerusalem. But do not worry. That is a burden heaven took upon itself, as only heaven can. And will, even to this very day.

The Miracle of Chance Encounters

Angels and Other Strangers
Katherine Paterson

Minutes after the letter came from Arlene, Jacob set out walking for Washington. He wondered how long it would take him to get there. Before the truck died, he could make it in an hour, but he'd never tried to walk it. At sixty he knew that he didn't have the endurance that he had once had, but he was still a strong man. Perhaps he could get there by morning if he kept a steady pace. Or if he could at least reach a place where there was a bus, he could ride as far as the few bills in his pocket could take him.

Arlene needed him, so he would go to her if he had to walk every step of the way. Arlene, his baby granddaughter, whom it seemed as if he had only just stopped bouncing on his knee, was going to have a baby herself. She was alone and scared in the city and wanted her granddaddy, so he had put on his dead wife's overcoat and then his own and started out. The two coats protected him from the wet snow, but his wife's was too small and cut under his arms. "I'm coming, Arlene baby," he said to the country road. "I'm going to be with you for Christmas."

How wonderful it would be, thought Jacob, if someone stopped and offered him a ride. Occasionally a car would pass, even on this almost deserted stretch. Once he almost raised his arm to try to wave one down, but thought better of it. Who would give a ride to a black man on a lonely road? He could hope in the Lord, but he'd better rely on his own two feet. No rest, as the Good Book said, for the weary.

In Washington, Julia Thompson was humming as she worked. Why was she so happy? Because she had two beautiful children and a loving husband. Because Walter, her husband, would be singing at the Christmas Eve service, and she always felt so proud and was thrilled by his voice. Because it was nearly Christmas. Yes, of course, all those things, but, hallelujah, it was the first Christmas since she'd known Walter that she hadn't had to deal with his Aunt Patty.

Aunt Patty was Walter's only living relative. Some respect was due her for his sake, but nothing ever went quite right with Aunt Patty. The best years were the ones when she had simply grumbled her way through the celebration, taking the edge off everyone else's enjoyment. But the last three years, she'd managed to orchestrate a series of disasters, though how could you blame an old lady for falling down on the church walk just before Christmas Eve service and having to be rushed to the hospital with a broken hip? Perhaps Aunt Patty should have known enough not to give a two-year-old a teddy bear with button eyes which he could and would immediately pull out and swallow, but she had not known, and it had meant that they had spent Christmas Day with Kevin in the emergency room. Last year, despite Julia's apprehension, everything had gone well, until they, with great excitement, told her the news that they were expecting another child. Aunt Patty, who had never before revealed a social conscience, suddenly burst into a lament for all the starving people in the world. Here they were, gorging themselves and daring to be happy, while at the same time producing still another baby to crowd out the hungry millions.

But this year, despite Walter's urgings, Aunt Patty had decided not to make the thirty-mile trip into the city. The weather was uncertain, and her bursitis had been acting up. Julia cleaned the house and shopped and baked with an energy she hadn't possessed since before Jenny was born. She even had strength left over to take the children on long walks and read aloud to Kevin. It was going to be a wonderful Christmas.

Julia put the baby down for a nap and then took Kevin up on her own bed and began reading to him. Ordinarily, Kevin loved being read to, but today he squirmed and wriggled straight through "The Night Before Christmas."

"My, you're fidgety," she said.

"Little boys are supposed to be fidgety," he said with dignity.

She hugged him close. "Now this is the story from the Bible about when Jesus was born. Try to listen, all right?"

"All right."

She read him the story of Mary and Joseph coming down from Nazareth to Bethlehem, stopping to explain about the taxes, the crowded inn, and the manger, going on to the shepherds in the field.

" 'And, lo, the angel of the Lord came upon them, and the glory of the Lord'—well, it's like a great light, Kevin—'shone round about them: and they were sore afraid. And the angel said unto them, Fear not . . . ' "

"Why were they afraid, Mommy?"

"I don't know—I guess the light and the strangeness. They'd never seen a real angel before."

He seemed satisfied. She read on, and since he was beginning to nod, she finished the whole chapter in a quiet voice until he was sound asleep. Julia propped pillows around him and went into the kitchen to clean up the lunch things and get ready for the evening. It was then that she discovered that they had no tangerines. Perhaps she was being silly, Kevin was only four and Jenny scarcely five months, but a Christmas stocking without a tangerine in the toe seemed somehow incomplete, and Julia was determined that this be a perfect Christmas. She got Becky the teen-ager from next door to baby-sit long enough to let her drive to the grocery store to pick up a few. She was home within twenty minutes.

"Everything quiet?" she asked the sitter.

"Sure. Fine. Your aunt called."

Julia's heart sank. "She said to tell you she'd changed her mind and would Mr. Thompson please come pick her up."

Julia should have asked Becky to stay with the children and gone then and there to get Aunt Patty, but she didn't. She paid Becky a dollar and sent her home before she tried to figure out what to do. Could she pretend she never got the message? No. She dialed Walter's office, looking at her watch as she did so. It was now three thirty. If he could leave Washington right away, he could drive the thirty-odd miles to Bethel, pick up Aunt Patty, and get back in time for his rehearsal. But when his secretary finally answered, it was to say that there had been an accident in the plant in Virginia, and that Walter had gone out to see about it. If he called in, she would have him call home.

That settled it. It was too late. There was no way to get Aunt Patty today, unless— Reluctantly she dialed the neighbors. No, Becky had already gone out with friends. She'd tried, Julia told herself. She really had. No one would expect her to put two sleeping children in the car and drive halfway across Maryland in bad weather.

The phone rang. "Julia?" It was, of course, Aunt Patty. "I want you just to forget my message. You mustn't bother Walter about me at such a busy time. It looks like snow anyhow. It would be ridiculous to come all the way out here."

Kevin came padding down the hall in his sock feet. "Who's that, Mommy?" he asked, still half asleep.

"Aunt Patty," Julia said.

"Aunt Patty!" His face lit up. "She's coming for Christmas!"

"Now I don't want you to feel bad," Aunt Patty was saying. "Just forget all about me and have a wonderful—"

"Aunt Patty," Julia broke in wearily, "we'll be there to get you as soon as we can."

There was a silence at the other end of the line. "Well, I think it's ridiculous to try to make it out here in this weather, but. . . . Well, all right. Since you insist."

Julia woke the baby and bundled both children into the car. It was already getting dark and snowing lightly, but she couldn't hon-

estly say that the roads were dangerous. Even driving slowly, she should have plenty of time to get out to Aunt Patty's house in the country and back in time for the service. Of course she hadn't counted on the crowded interstate on Christmas Eve afternoon. They alternately crawled and sat, motors idling, horns honking about them.

On the back seat Jenny slept while Kevin chattered away. He was so excited about getting his Aunt Patty that he sang songs about it, substituting Aunt Patty for Santa Claus. I ought to deserve some credit, Julia thought, that despite everything, I've never turned Kevin against her.

It was nearly five before they were off the main highway and moving at a decent rate of speed. If the visibility had been really poor or the road icy, Julia would have turned around for home even then. But there was no way she could escape this journey now without disappointing her little boy and making herself feel like Scrooge incarnate.

They were dangerously low on gas, but there was a station just this side of Aunt Patty's place where she could fill up, so she pushed on. When they got there, though, the station was closed for the holiday, so she drove on to Aunt Patty's house.

"Just wait with Jenny, Kevin. I'll run in and get Aunt Patty, and we'll be right back." She dashed from the driveway to the back door and banged. It was bitter cold, though the snow was slackening. She tried the door. It fell open. "Aunt Patty?" she called in the hallway. One of Aunt Patty's cats came bouncing down the steps, meowing menacingly. "Aunt Patty?" She was seized with a sudden panic that the old woman might be lying somewhere in the house, ill or worse. Then her eye fell on the note on the kitchen table.

"Walter," it said. "I've just run up to Gertrude's for a minute. You can pick me up there or wait here for me. I won't be long. Love." Walter, were he here, might know who Gertrude was, but Julia had no notion. She wouldn't even know how to look her up in the phone book.

She went back to the car.

"Where's Aunt Patty?" asked Kevin. Where indeed was Aunt Patty?

"She went to see a friend and is coming back soon. We'll go put some gas in the car. By the time we get back, she'll probably be here."

"Why'd she go away? Didn't she know we were coming?"

Julia started the engine and began backing down the drive. She was not going to ruin Christmas by losing her temper.

"Why, Mommy?"

"I don't know, Kevin. She didn't tell me."

"Did you see her?"

"No. She left a note." Addressed to Walter, naturally.

"What did the note say?"

"She just said she was going out for a few minutes and would be right back."

"Why?"

"Kevin!"

"Why'd you yell at me, Mommy?"

"Please, Kevin. I've got to watch the road." Where in the world was the nearest gas station? One that would still be open at five thirty on Christmas Eve? There was a housing development with a shopping center somewhere about—she had driven there once with Walter—if she could remember the road to take to cut over to it. Aunt Patty's road was a narrow two-lane country road with very few houses. The windshield wipers pushed the snow aside, and she sat hunched forward, peering out into the path of the headlights, not daring to glance at the gas gauge.

In the darkness, nothing looked familiar. She rarely came out here, and when she did, Walter always drove. She should have stayed and waited for Aunt Patty, but it was too late now to try to turn around and get back.

"Why are you stopping the car, Mommy?"

Julia put her head down on the wheel. She was not going to panic. She had two children to look after. She had to think clearly.

The baby woke up and began to scream.

"The baby woke up, Mommy."

"I know, sweetheart."

"Why'd you stop the car?"

"Don't get upset, Kevin. We've just run out of gas. Everything will be all right. Just don't get upset."

"I'm not upset. The baby's upset. I'm fidgety."

"Well, you can get out of your seat for a while." She reached back and undid his seat belt. He clambered happily into the front seat.

"Oh, tuna fish," he cursed, four-year-old style. "It's stopped snowing."

Julia took Jenny out of the car bed. One thing at a time. First, the baby must be fed. As she nursed the baby, she began to sing to entertain Kevin, who was jealous that his sister could have her supper while he could not.

They were singing about glories streaming from heaven afar when Kevin spotted the light ahead. "Look, Mommy!"

Jacob had first seen the headlights come quickly over a rise far down the road and then as quickly disappear. He kept walking, swinging his huge flashlight as he went, expecting them to reappear at any moment. Not that it mattered. The car was heading the wrong way for him anyhow, even if by some miracle it was someone who would consider giving him a ride. At least it had stopped snowing. Just then the beam of his flashlight caught a car sitting in the darkness. There were people inside. He hesitated a moment. What if it were a trick? For himself he didn't mind dying. Lord knew he was ready to go, but Arlene needed him now. He had to get to Washington. Yet here, perhaps, was somebody else in need. He started across the road, heading for the driver's side of the car.

Look, Mommy!" Kevin said again. "Glory streams from heaven afar." A strong bright light moved over the rise and down the hill toward them. Julia stopped singing and watched it come. Finally, behind the light, she could make out the tall bulging shadow of a man. She checked quickly to make sure all the doors were locked, took the baby off her breast, and straightened her clothes with a shaking hand. The light was coming straight for her window. Her eyes blinked to shut out the brightness, and when she opened them, a huge black face, which seemed to fill the side

window of the small car, was there within inches of her cheek. She pulled back. The man tapped on the window with a worn brown glove that showed the tips of his fingers, and said something through the glass. Julia squeezed the baby tighter and stared straight ahead.

Kevin leaned across her and banged the glass. "Hi!" he said.

"Hi yourself."

Out of the corner of her eye Julia could see the black face smiling broadly. The chin was covered with silver bristles and several teeth were missing. She tried to grab at Kevin to shush him.

"Need some help?" This time the man was shouting as though to make sure she could hear him plainly through the window, but she refused to turn her head.

"Mommy, why don't you answer the nice man?"

"Shh, Kevin. We don't know what he wants."

"He wants to know if we need some help."

The man leaned close to the glass and shouted again. "Don't be afraid, little lady."

"You hear that, Mommy?"

"Kevin, please."

"But, Mommy, he said, 'Don't be afraid!' That's what *angels* say."

"Kevin, no!"

But before she could catch him, Kevin had slid across the seat, pulled up the button, opened the door, and jumped out of the car. The man immediately started around to meet him.

"Don't you touch my child!" Julia screamed, twisting awkwardly from under the wheel, still clutching the baby.

"You don't want him running out into the road, do you, lady?"

"No. No. Thank you." She took Kevin's hand.

"I saw your car and figured you was in trouble."

There was no way to ignore him now. But she had to be careful. He was over six feet tall and obviously strong. The police-pamphlet directions flashed across her brain: *Be sure to look carefully at your assailant so you can give an accurate description to the police later.* If there was a later. Oh, God, don't let him hurt me. Don't let him hurt the children.

"We run out of gas," said Kevin.

Why was she so afraid of him? He, Jacob, who had never willfully hurt the least one of God's creatures—couldn't she tell by looking at him that he only wanted to help? Even the child could see that. He stretched out his hand to put it on the boy's head, but seeing the look in the woman's eyes, he brought it back.

"Your old car's got a empty belly, huh?"

The boy giggled. "Me, too," he said. "I haven't even had my supper."

"Well, we gotta do something about that. I passed a gas station a while back," Jacob said to the woman. "You don't have a can, do you?"

She shook her head. She seemed to be shivering.

"You better get back in the car and try to stay warm." He turned and started back up the hill, sighing as he retraced the descent of a few minutes before. It seemed to have grown steeper. But, at least, praise the Lord, the snow had stopped and the sky was clearing.

"Wait," she called after him. "You'll need some money."

"I got some," Jacob said. He didn't want to waste time and energy going back down the hill.

Suppose he never came back? Would they grow cold and sleepy and freeze out here in the middle of nowhere on Christmas Eve? Well, Aunt Patty, you will have certainly beaten your own record this year—even Christmas morning in the emergency room will pale in comparison. And then suppose he did come back? What did he want? He could have just taken her purse and run, if money was what he wanted. But of course it was the car he was after, so he could get away faster—but she tried not to think of that.

"I think we should sing some more songs," Kevin said. "I might forget about my tummy."

Julia was glad for the diversion. They sang through every carol she knew, even la-la-ing through unfamiliar verses. Then they sang all the songs on Kevin's favorite records, then another round of Christmas carols. Until at long last they saw the light coming over the hill.

"Here comes the glory light," said Kevin.

This time when the man came to her window, she rolled it down. "Would you hold the flashlight for me while I pour the gas in?" he asked.

Trembling, she laid Jenny down in the car bed and went around to the tank. He handed her his big torch, which she tried to hold steady as he poured.

"Well, thank you," Julia said when he had finished, keeping her voice cool. "Let me pay you something for all your trouble."

Jacob looked at her. She was going to give him some money and drive off. He had given her nearly an hour of his time and far more of his energy than he could spare. There was no way she could pay him for that. But she had already gone to the front seat and gotten her purse, the little boy scampering around her at every step.

"That's all right," he said. "Forget it."

She stuck a few bills out at him. "But I owe you for the gas."

"I—uh—do need to return the can. If you could give me a ride down the road and back. . . ."

She nodded.

He could tell by her eyes that she didn't want him in her car but, Lord, she owed him that much. He decided to ignore her eyes.

"Well, old man," he said to the child, "let's see if we can get this old buggy going." He took the boy around and put him in his seat, letting the child tell him how to buckle the belt, and then climbed into the front seat.

The woman put her purse down between them and buckled herself in. Jacob looked down at her purse and then realized she had caught him looking. He quickly shifted his gaze. "Just down the road a couple miles or so," he said.

Within ten minutes they were at the lighted station. She gave the can back to the attendant and asked him to fill the tank. She saw his eyes question the presence of the man on the seat beside her. Should she try to signal for help? It seemed too foolish. The man had done nothing except try to help her—so far. She at least owed him a ride home on this freezing night.

"We come to get my Aunt Patty to take her home for Christmas." Oh, Kevin.

"Is that a fact? Where's your home, old man?"

Don't answer him, Kevin. But of course Kevin, who had memorized his full address at nursery school, recited it in a proud singsong: "Thirteen-oh-six Essex Street Northwest, Washington, D.C. Two-oh-oh-one-six."

"My, you're one smart boy."

"I know," said Kevin.

I could get a ride all the way to Washington tonight, Jacob said to himself. All I have to do is ask. But he couldn't make himself say the words. If the woman had seemed in the least bit friendly, the least bit trusting, he would have asked her. But how could he ask a favor of a person who thought he was going to grab her purse or hurt her kids?

She had started the car and was pulling out of the station. "Where shall I let you off?" she asked.

It was his chance to tell her. She owed him something, didn't she? And Arlene was waiting, not even knowing if he had gotten her letter.

"Just down the road," he mumbled. "Just anywhere."

They drove past the place where they had met, but he gave no sign of wanting to be let out, so Julia drove on. She couldn't just stop in the middle of nowhere and order him out. What should she do? They went on until she could see Aunt Patty's house ablaze with light. Aunt Patty was home. Thank God for small blessings.

"Here's where Aunt Patty lives," Kevin told the stranger.

"Is that a fact?"

The problem of how to get Aunt Patty without leaving the children alone in the car with the man solved itself. Aunt Patty came rushing out of the house, coat and suitcase flying. She had obviously been watching for the car. When she saw Julia at the wheel, she was furious. "Where have you been?" she demanded. "You're going to make me miss the music."

Julia opened her mouth to defend herself, but at the same moment her passenger got out of the car. He stood there tall and straight against the starry winter sky.

"Mercy!" Aunt Patty screamed. "What in the world?"

"He's our angel, Aunt Patty. Our Christmas angel."

"Don't be ridiculous, Kevin."

Ridiculous indeed! All Julia's fears evaporated in a puff of anger. How dare Aunt Patty call it ridiculous? The man had been an angel. She leaned across the seat and called out, "Would you mind squeezing in back with the children?"

Even in the darkness she thought she could see him smile.

"Get in, Aunt Patty," she commanded, "or you'll make us miss the music."

A little farther down the road she turned to him. "How far can I take you?"

"I need to go all the way to Washington," he said.

"Oh, goody!" cried Kevin. "Then you can go to church with us! We never had a real angel in our church before."

He patted the boy's knee. "Can't make it this time, old man," he said. "I got to go see this lonesome little girl. Cheer her up for Christmas."

"Angels are really busy, aren't they?"

Jacob laughed, a great rich sound which filled the car. "Yeah," he said. "We keep busy, but it's mighty pleasant work."

Aunt Patty may have said something that sounded like "ridiculous," but Julia joyfully chose to ignore it. This was going to be a perfect Christmas.

Christmas on the Moor
Elizabeth Goudge

1

Ever since the mist had come down Martin had kept a careful silence. His mind was bursting with the things he wanted to say to Maria, things about the superiority of a man's judgement, and obeying husbands and so on, but they had only been married for ten months and he still tried not to say the things. Nevertheless, since the whole adventure was her fault entirely, he could not help thinking them.

Maria was not country-bred and when he had brought her home to the old farmhouse under the shoulder of the moor, that had been his father's and his grandfather's and was now his, she had not found it easy to adjust herself. She had missed the parties she had been used to, and her sisters and their fun. She and Martin had no carriage, only the gig and a couple of riding horses, which was all a young gentleman farmer could expect to have in the 1800s. At first she was happy enough for the beauty of the country took her wild heart by storm and she loved exploring it on horseback, but the baby started to come and Martin got nervous and would not let her ride any more. And then the autumn closed down, with rain and gales from the sea, and gay and pleasure loving as she was she got depressed and restless. She must go home for Christmas, she said, and Martin must come too, for she would not go without him when it was the first Christmas of their married life. He said he couldn't leave the farm. She said he could. They had one of their flaming rows, for they were both high-spirited, and then one of their glorious reconciliations, for they were still deeply in love, and Maria won, because though she was five years younger than Martin, twenty to his twenty-five, she was just that much more determined on her own way than he was; though he was determined too, and he kept to it that they leave home on Christmas Eve and return on December twenty-eighth. Three full days at her papa's, but no more. He would not trust the farm hands with his precious beasts a moment longer than that. She knew that particular set of his firm lips and conceded the minor point, having won the major one, and honour being now more or less equally satisfied they became as excited as children as they made their preparations.

It wasn't far to go to the country town where Maria had been born, ten miles over the moor or eighteen miles round by the turnpike road. They would go the long way round, Martin decided. It was safer, with the weather uncertain and the baby due in a month. Maria arched her eyebrows and shot him a wicked sparkling look at the word "safer," which was to her what a red rag is to a bull. If anyone told her to go through the gap in the hedge rather than over the gate she set her horse instantly at the gate. A suggestion that it would be safer to close the window in a thunderstorm made her immediately open it as wide as possible. But Martin had not been married to Maria quite long enough yet to bear this fact continually in mind, and anyway he was lighting his pipe at the time and scarcely noticed her look. He was to remember it later.

Christmas Eve dawned sunlit and sparkling, and almost as warm as spring. They put the small corded trunk packed with their best clothes and the presents for the family under the seat of the gig and settled themselves happily together beneath the plaid rug. Maria looked enchanting in her crimson fur-trimmed pelisse and velvet bonnet. She was not beautiful, for her nose was too large and her cleft chin too resolute, but her brilliant laughing eyes made her seem so. She was a brown girl, her dusky hair springing wirily from her broad forehead and her golden skin clear and rose-tinted with her perfect health. Her pregnancy had not sapped her vitality in the least. She was looking forward to going home again in a month's time and having the baby with Mamma and Dr. Fothergill in devoted attendance. She loved the old doctor, brusque and out-spoken though he was. It would be impossible to have a baby with-out him.

They bowled along through the village and swept out into the turnpike in fine style, for the grey horse Beauty was as high-spirited as his owners. The gig, new at the time of their marriage, had yellow wheels that flashed as though the sun were tangled up in them. Martin's holly-green greatcoat and curly beaver hat set at a jaunty angle were becoming to his flaming red head and freckled, sun-tanned handsomeness. He kept his back straight and drove with dash and skill. Maria adored driving with him and never loved him so much as when they bowled along together like this with the wind whistling past them and their glowing bodies warm together under the rug.

To the right the moor lifted in fold upon fold towards the sky, the tawny, dead bracken gold when the sun touched it, the withered heather wine-dark under the dry-stone walls. Those who lived be-neath it could never forget the moor. It was always subtly present to their thoughts and dreams and they glanced towards it con-stantly, sometimes with a slight uneasiness, as men eye a mounting storm on the horizon. To the left was the good and gentle land, with its round green hills and fields where the sheep were feeding, its deep woods and ferny lanes.

A cock crowed loudly behind them, where a farmhouse stood crookedly among orchard trees, and they were startled, for they were looking towards the moor. "The cock, that is the trumpet to the morn," quoted Maria, who had been well educated and knew poetry by heart.

"It's afternoon," said Martin, who was literal-minded and imper-vious to Shakespeare. "We've started late, you know. All because you couldn't find your fan and wouldn't pack till the last moment. Women!"

But he was still good-humoured and looked down at her with his grey-green eyes up in amusement and his wide mouth curling up at the corners. Maria laughed back at him and went on airing her

Shakespearian knowledge, just to provoke him.

> "Some say that ever 'gainst that season comes
> Wherein our Saviour's birth is celebrated,
> The bird of dawning singeth all night long;
> And then, they say, no spirit can walk abroad;
> The nights are wholesome; then no planets strike,
> No fairy takes, nor witch hath power to charm,
> So hallow'd and so gracious is the time."

To please her he was duly provoked. "Moonshine," he scoffed. "If you want to gabble by rote like a parrot why not get a few recipes by heart? Squab pie and dumplings. Dinner wouldn't be so late if you didn't waste so much time with your nose in a cook book. My mother made wonderful squab pie."

She let that pass, and went back to the subject of moonshine. "How do you know there are no fairies or witches? You don't know." She looked up at the great brooding presence of the moor. "How do you know what lives up there? Whenever you've taken me there, though we've never been far, I've felt them. Haven't you?"

Martin looked down into her eager face, raised to his, and so full of laughter that he did not know if she was mocking or serious. That was one of the enchanting things about her; he never quite knew what she was really thinking. She was mysterious. He laughed without answering. Yet as a boy, birds'-nesting up there, he had felt them. Boys, he supposed, imagined things. "Good and bad," went on Maria. "But not bad ones to-day or to-morrow. Shakespeare meant the bad spirits. They've gone. They daren't be about at Christmas. But the good ones are about more than ever."

They drove on and came to the place where the narrow lane to the moors forked away from the turnpike. "Turn right, Martin," she said imperiously.

He should have known better than to pull up. He should have driven straight on as fast as he could. He knew quite well that if he gave ground at the start he was likely to lose the whole sparring match. He lost it now, though it was hotly contested. She said it was madness to go the long way round when it was miles shorter

over the moor. He reminded her of the hazards of the moor, and could have reminded her of nothing more likely to harden her determination. She spoke of the beauty of the day and its extraordinary clarity, and looking up at the splendour above her was suddenly wild to be in it and of it. He'd always promised to take her right up over the moor and he never had. He would one day, he said. But what she wanted was never any good to Maria in the form of a distant promise. She wanted it now or not at all. What could happen? Was he afraid? She hated cowards. Hadn't he told her he knew the moor like the palm of his hand? This was a boast that he had made when he was courting her. He had boasted of much in those days, he had been so wild to win her, and not all his boasts had been strictly true. Afraid? He flicked his whip over Beauty's back and set him at a canter up the lane.

They drove up and up, the deep banks changing to dry-stone walls, and all about them the great views widened out. Down below the gentle land looked flat as a child's counterpane, sinking to unreality. This, now, was what was real, this world that was lifted up, the stark hills and the hidden valleys musical with streams, the clear cold air and the silence. They seemed the only living creatures in this world but they could not feel that it belonged to them, as a deserted meadow down below would have seemed their own. They might presently belong to it, but not yet. It held them in the hollow of its hand, watching them, but the hand had not yet closed upon them.

But they were enjoying themselves. They spoke little but they looked at each other often and smiled. Down below the surface eddies their love for each other was already beginning to cut a steady channel for itself and to flow strong and deep. Up here they were aware that their quarrels, which had secretly worried them both, did not matter. They would subside in time. What each wanted of the other was secretly already in being. They drove steadily uphill, into the woods and out of them, over the old stone bridges and along the banks of the racing streams, and were too absorbed in each other to notice that the sun had gone in and the sky was veiled. When the mist finally came down it took them by surprise. But Martin was quite sure he knew the way and repeated the boast about the palm of his hand.

But as they went on he grew silent, and angry with Maria because he had not had the strength of mind to keep on along the turnpike. He was getting very anxious about her and the more uneasy he was the more annoyed with her he became. He did not look at her but now and then she looked at him, at his strong sullen mouth and fine hands on the reins, and now and then she laughed inside herself. They were lost, of course, but it was fun to be lost with Martin. Presently he would stop being annoyed and then they would be able to enjoy it together.

They jolted over a stone in the road and a wheel came off. It was the most extraordinary thing to happen and was beyond Martin's comprehension. They had been going very slowly and Maria clung to the side and was not hurt at all, and laughed at Martin's grave face as he helped her down and held her for a minute or two in his arms. "One of the bad ones must have done it," she said. "The last thing it did before it went into hiding over Christmas. Don't worry, Martin. Take Beauty out of the gig and I'll ride him, and you can walk beside me. We'll soon be there."

"We won't," said Martin. "We're lost, you know."

"Yes, I know, but we're on some sort of a road and it must lead somewhere. To a farm or village. We've only got to follow it."

He did not tell her for how many miles one could follow these tracks over the moor and not get anywhere. He lifted her on Beauty and wrapped the rug about her, and took one of the lanterns from the gig, and now they were no longer silent but laughed and talked together in case the other should be feeling low-spirited. Then they fell silent again, for it was growing dark and late, the mist was thicker than ever and instead of the track going downhill towards the good and gentle land it was going up and up. Martin stopped and lit the lantern and Maria bent down and tried to see his face. "Martin," she said. "I'm sorry. It was my fault."

He looked up and smiled at her. "My fault too. We've been a couple of fools together."

"But together," she said. "Are you very tired?"

"No, love. Are you?"

"Of course not," she said indignantly, but looking up at her in the lantern light he saw that there were dark shadows under her

eyes and his heart seemed to turn over. Ten minutes later she gave a sudden glad cry. "Look, Martin! A garden wall!"

He stopped with an exclamation of astonishment and held up the lantern. The wall was old, buttressed and strong. Inside was perhaps one of those moor gardens, sheltered from the wind, where magnolia trees grew against the south wall, and in summer herbs and flowers were all knotted together to make a paradise for bees. But it was odd that he had not seen it before, and odd that they should have apparently left the track without noticing it, for under the wall and beneath their feet was only the mist-drenched grass. "We'll follow along, Maria," he said joyously. "There must be something here."

They moved on and came to a splendid old archway in the wall. It had iron gates in it and they were hospitably open; yet the steep carriage-way beyond was almost lost among the brambles and rhododendrons that had grown across it. Holding the lantern high, Martin led Beauty through its tunnel-like windings. He could not see the trees that arched above them but he knew they must be there because of the soft drip from overhead.

The way widened out suddenly and the glimmer of a white shape startled them, but it was only the stone figure of a boy with a dolphin standing in the midst of a stone basin where once there had been a fountain. Beyond it broken steps led up to a terrace and they could just see a shuttered house and a front door with pillars on either side and a fanlight over it. No light came from the door but it was open.

It seemed quite natural to them both that Martin should help Maria down and tether Beauty to a vast japonica tree that grew beside the fountain. Then hand in hand they mounted the steps and went inside the house. It seemed empty and dark but the lantern light gleamed on the panelling and the gracious sweep of the staircase beyond. Several doors opened out of the hall but only one was ajar. They pushed it and went in. Inside was a small parlour and it was partly furnished. There were branched candlesticks on the mantelpiece, with candles in them festooned with cobwebs, and an old cracked French mirror between them. A brocade sofa, torn now but once rose-coloured and lovely, was drawn to the empty basket grate. Maria dropped down upon it and Martin covered her with the rug. Then he lit the candles. It was a beautiful room, its panelling painted pale apple-green. The paint was peeling off in places and there were damp stains on the ceiling, but still it was beautiful.

"You need a fire, Maria," said Martin, for she was shivering violently beneath the rug. "I'll go round to the back and see if I can find some dry wood."

"There's Beauty," said Maria.

"I'll take him with me. There may be a stable there."

He found a stable at the back, and the door was open. In one of the loose boxes there was hay in the manger and a bucket of water. Martin was somehow not surprised and Beauty was well content. In a corner of the stable there was a pile of dry logs, oak and beech, and fircones and a couple of sacks. He filled both and went round to the front door again, bent almost double beneath his load. "Soon have a fire, sweetheart," he said gaily as he lowered the sacks beside the hearth, and he kindled one easily with flint and tinder. It was surprising how quickly the flame leaped up the chimney, orange and blue and sea-green, and when the warmth stole out into the room it brought a fragrance with it. Yet it struck him that Maria was being oddly silent. He had expected admiration and congratulation. He looked round over his shoulder and saw her with enormous dark eyes in a blanched face. She had taken off her bonnet and her dark hair was in a tangle on her shoulders. Yet when he smiled at her she gave him an impish grin.

He dropped on his knees beside her and took her hands and his face was as white as hers. He looked so like a terrified schoolboy who has seen a ghost that she laughed, though the laugh had a crack in the middle. "It must have been jolting over the stone, when the wheel came off," she said. "Don't look so scared, Martin. There must be a village or this house would not be here. Take the lantern and go and find it, love. There are always midwives in villages."

"But I can't leave you alone," he said.

"But you must, you silly. Nothing can happen to me. A first baby takes hours. Go on, love. What else can we do?"

He crushed her hands nearly to pulp in his, then released them and got up. Then he took the lantern and went. She was right. There was nothing else to do.

He followed a grass-grown road down through the dripping woods until it forked. Then he stopped and he felt nearly crazed, for there was no signpost, no glimmer of light either way to tell him where the village was. Yet the mist was thinning slightly and he thought he saw a slight movement to the left. "Hi, you there!" he shouted, and strode forward with his lantern. Yes, it was a man, a tall old Negro with white hair. For just a moment he was vividly aware of dark eyes, incredibly gentle, the flash of a compassionate smile and the gesture of a hand, and then he was following the old man down through the woods. They did not speak, for the other was always just ahead of him, not clearly seen through the mist but never difficult to follow. Yet the way through the woods he could not have followed had he not been led, for it twisted and turned and at times was almost lost beneath the undergrowth. It seemed hours to him before the trees thinned and he heard a cock crowing, and then they came out into a deep lane and there were the lights of the village down below. After that he ran and soon he was thundering on a cottage door. It opened in a moment and he was pouring out his story to the kindly woman who stood there with such comfortable stolidity. He had forgotten the old Negro.

2

When she was alone Maria tried her best not to be terrified. She had thought she did not know what it was to be afraid but then she had never had a baby before. Toothache had been the worst she had known. Never anything like this, rhythmic pain roaring up at her and dragging back like waves breaking, and in the dark curve of each wave as it broke over her there was this fear. She would not have been so terrified if she had not been alone. If Mamma and Dr. Fothergill had been with her she would not have minded. Or if Martin had been able to stay with her they could have held hands and it would not have been so bad. But Martin was out in the night and he might never find the village. He might fall and hurt himself and not come back. Then she and the baby would die here. They would die without Dr. Fothergill. It was the old doctor she wanted so badly, more than Mamma or Martin. Once she thought she heard his step in the hall and she called out to him, "Doctor Fothergill! The baby's coming. Please come quickly!" But he did not come and she remembered that he could not possibly come. He was miles away. She and the baby were alone in this empty house and they would die. She knew she was making no sound but inside herself she heard her voice crying out in panic. "No! No! No!" she was crying. "I won't die. I won't."

She sat up on the sofa and pushed the heavy hair back from her forehead. "No," she said aloud. "I won't. And I won't scream. It's Christmas Eve. Martin will come back."

She lay down again and found she had controlled the terror. Or else something outside herself had conquered it. Was it the room? Shabby and cobwebbed though it was it had a safe and friendly look. The candles were not burnt out yet and the small flames swaying in the draught and then righting themselves were like flowers blown in the wind. The reflected firelight glowed warmly in the panelling. The last great wave, the one that had brought her terror nearly to screaming pitch, had dragged back and another had not come upon her. Nature was resting and she was at peace. She began to feel sleepy in the warmth of the fire, and she did not feel alone. She was not alone. She slipped her hand under her cheek and shut her eyes and murmured drowsily, "I am not alone."

In her dream the fire was still warm and glowing and the candles burning, but they were not swaying in the draught because long rose-coloured curtains hung over the shutters. There were no cobwebs and the pale leaf-green walls were fresh and clean. Beaupots of flowers stood against them, and chairs with slender gold legs. Miniatures hung on the walls, and garlanded shepherds and shepherdesses stood on the mantelpiece. There was a harpsichord between the two tall windows and a woman sat before it, her fingers running up and down over the keys. She was enjoying herself, for her lips were parted in a smile and she swayed very slightly to her music, her head bent, absorbed in it. The skirt of her deep blue silk dress, the colour of bluebells when they are still in bud, was so full that it swirled all round her on the floor and hid her feet. There was white lace at her throat and white hair was piled up on her head, though she was not old. But she was not young either, not like Maria. Her smiling mouth was not a girl's mouth, and no girl could have played the harpsichord as she was doing. The gay lambent music was like a shower of spring rain when the sun is out, or like a family of young robins singing together. It was like a candled Christmas-tree or a child laughing. Maria laughed as she listened to it and she thought it was her child laughing, her child safely born and grown and clapping his hands at the candled tree. "See how pretty he is," she cried to the woman. "Look how he laughs at the tree!" But the room was growing darker and the music silent. Instead of the rippling notes she heard only the frou-frou of a woman's skirts as she came swiftly across the polished floor. "Don't let me wake till I see you," Maria said to her. "Don't let me wake till I see your face."

But she could not hold the dream and when she woke the cobwebbed room was as before and there was no one there. Yet still she felt she was not alone. She lay quietly relaxed, still hearing the laughter of the child. Far away in the distance she heard a cock crow, and she smiled.

3

Everyone had a greeting for Dr. Fothergill as he drove down the street in his battered old gig; and for everyone he had a cheery smile, a wave of the hand or a facetious remark. He was a character. No one could visualize the little town without him and no one wanted to or ever tried to. He seemed as much a permanent feature of the place as the weathercock on top of the church tower. He was old, people supposed, though they did not know how old. His hair was grey and his rosy weather-beaten face deeply seamed, but he was stout and robust and his hearty laugh could be heard almost from one end of the town to the other. He held himself so well that it was generally supposed that he wore corsets, and possibly he did, for he was a dressy man. He affected an eyeglass, the latest in cravats and waistcoats and curly-brimmed hats, and even on his country rounds he wore his jewellery; his gold watch with its dangling seals and a couple of fine rings. And he always seemed to carry a good deal of loose money in his pockets. Whenever he was considering a case he would stand in front of the fireplace with his legs apart and his hands in his pockets and jingle the coins. Patients knew just how ill they were by the amount of jingling that went on. He was an excellent doctor. Each patient was as important to him as though he had no other and neither weather nor distance nor any trouble of his own had ever caused him to refuse a call for help.

Nevertheless he was glad to be on his way home now to his warm fireside and his good stout wife, Jemima, and he hoped in heaven's name that he would not be called out over Christmas. There were no babies due just now, for that young hussy Maria was not expecting hers for some weeks yet, and he had done his best to put all his old folks into pickle for a day or two. With any luck they should last. His thoughts turned fondly to roast goose and plum pudding, his pipe and a locked surgery door.

"Doctor! Doctor!"

It was the high cry of distress that he knew only too well. The ragged little boy came running across the road to him, dodging under the very noses of the horses, and cursing profusely he reined his own horse in beside the curb.

"What do you want, boy?" he demanded angrily, as the urchin leaped up on the step and hung there clinging to the side of the gig.

"Farmer Mudge, sir, up at Longbarton Farm, took terrible bad."

Longbarton Farm was up on the moor, an isolated place and a lonely ride to get there. "Mudge!" said Dr. Fothergill. "What's the matter with him?"

"Dunno, doctor. But I was to say he's terrible bad."

"Blast him," said Dr. Fothergill, and then sticking in his eyeglass he had a good look at the small boy clinging to the side of the gig. "Who are you, boy? Never set eyes on you before. Who sent you?"

The boy's dark eyes stared up at him out of a blanched and

peaky face. "He's terrible bad, doctor," he pleaded huskily. Then he jumped down and dodged away through the traffic, dived down a side street and was lost to sight. "Must be one of the Mudge brood," thought Dr. Fothergill, as he whipped up his horse and drove on. Yet the Mudge brood were a healthy lot, with full stomachs and brown faces, and if the boy had been one of them he would have asked for a lift home. It was odd. He wouldn't go. No sir. It was Christmas Eve.

Yet at home, when he had clattered into his stable yard in a tearing rage, he flung the reins to his groom and shouted at him to saddle the strong cob he kept for his country rounds. Indoors he leaped upstairs two at a time and while he changed into his riding clothes he roared at Jemima, in the kitchen stuffing the goose, to bring him a hunk of bread and cheese and a glass of ale to the surgery. While he ate and drank she packed his saddle bags, as she had done so many times before, pausing every now and then to wipe her eyes, for though she had been a doctor's wife for forty years, and should have learnt resignation by this time, she had been looking forward to this Christmas. "Don't be a fool, Jemima," he growled at her. "I'll be back before morning."

"You'd better be," she sobbed. "It's a beautiful goose. John, if I've told you once I've told you a hundred times not to wear your gold watch and rings with your riding clothes. It's not suitable."

"Always have worn 'em and always shall," said Dr. Fothergill. He put his arm round her waist, gave her a smacking kiss and was gone. She heard him clatter out of the stable yard, burst into tears and went back to the goose. Luckily she was too absorbed in it to notice that the sunlight had gone and the sky was veiled.

Dr. Fothergill noticed it as he rode up into the hills. He would be mist-bound quite soon and he urged his horse forward. Noah was a good horse, and used to the moors, and they went at a good speed, but Dr. Fothergill still swore under his breath and vowed that if it turned out to be nothing but the colic he'd have something to say to Mudge.

An hour later he very nearly missed the farmhouse altogether. If Noah had not swerved to avoid the mounting block by the gate he would have missed it. He was thankful when at his knock the door opened and the warmth and light flowed out to him, but astonished beyond measure to have it opened by Farmer Mudge himself, stout and hearty as ever.

"Doctor!" ejaculated Farmer Mudge. "Whatever brings you here at this time of night?"

"Your severe illness," said Dr. Fothergill grimly. "I shall be obliged to you, Mudge, for an explanation." And he stepped forward into the warm kitchen, where a brood of happy children and a smiling mother were absorbing rabbit soup.

There was no explanation. Farmer Mudge had sent no message. He did not know the boy. Obviously some other farm had been meant. There was a muddle somewhere. One thing however Farmer Mudge did know and that was that the doctor must spend the night with them. Only a moor man would be able to find his way home in this mist.

"Only a moor man?" ejaculated Dr. Fothergill indignantly. "I'll have you know, Mudge, that I could find my way blindfold over the moor before you were born. Thank you, ma'am, I'll take a sup of that soup and then be off home to my wife. Christmas Eve, you know. She wants me at home."

The farmer tried again to dissuade him, for there was a fear at the back of his mind that he could not mention aloud. Failing, he offered to come with him, but this suggestion got Dr. Fothergill's back up to an alarming extent. "I know the moor like the palm of my hand," he exploded. "I've only to follow the road straight down. Well, a happy Christmas to you all and I never tasted better rabbit soup."

He fished up a handful of loose money from his pockets, gave the children sixpence all round, slapped his hat on his head and stumped away. The farmer saw him go with anxiety. But for his wife's grip on his coat tails he would have run to the stable for his own horse and followed after.

Half an hour later, after a somewhat anxious period of not admitting even to himself that he was not quite sure where he was, Dr. Fothergill ejaculated "Aha!" with pleasure and self-congratulation, for through the mist he could recognize a landmark that he knew, a parting of the ways where one path led down off the moor and the other branched uphill again to the right, and in spite of his boast that he knew the moor like the palm of his hand it was a way that he had never followed. His pleasure seemed to have communicated itself to Noah for the horse suddenly gave a sharp whinny of pleasure, almost as though he had seen another horse, trotted forward and swung round uphill to the right.

"You're wrong, Noah," said Dr. Fothergill, and tried to force the cob round again into the right path. But Noah would not go. He reared up when his master used the whip but he would not turn round. He stood with his legs splayed out, sweating with distress, his nostrils dilated, but he would not take the other path. Dr. Fothergill took off his hat and wiped his forehead. Had he made a mistake? Was he right off his proper track and was this branching of the ways not the one he knew but another? Suddenly he decided to trust Noah. He knew the wisdom of horses and of Noah in particular. "Have your own way then, lad," he said, and let the reins go slack.

Noah instantly started off uphill to the right, and though the mist was still thick and darkness was closing in he climbed at a good pace, as though sure of his way, and now and then he turned his head to the left and whinnied happily. He kept always to the right of the path. Several times Dr. Fothergill tried to coax him to the centre, where it was easier going, but he would not respond to the pressure on the bridle. He kept to the right.

It was the strangest ride Dr. Fothergill had ever taken. The mist decreased slightly, but the darkness increased. Sometimes they rode under the dripping darkness of trees, sometimes out in the open. Twice they came to a gate and Dr. Fothergill had to dismount and open it. Each time Noah moved confidently through, keeping to the right. Once he thought a village must be near, for he thought he heard a cock crowing. Then the path moved into a thick wood and went steeply uphill in darkness. But Noah had no difficulty in keeping to the path, and Dr. Fothergill himself, though he had not the faintest notion where he was, felt oddly secure and happy, as he had felt ever since he had yielded his will to Noah's. The wood ended and they rode under an archway in a stone wall, and up a carriage-drive, and at the foot of some steps, in front of a house where light showed through the chinks of the shutters of a downstairs room, Noah stopped abruptly. Dr. Fothergill dismounted, walked up the steps and across the terrace and knocked at the door. It was opened by Martin, holding a lantern in his hand. He looked haggard and distraught, his red hair rumpled and his eyes sunken in pits of shadow.

"I'm the doctor," said Dr. Fothergill calmly.

"The doctor!" Martin lowered the lantern and peered in the other man's face. "Dear God! Doctor Fothergill!" His hand shot out and gripped the doctor's shoulder. "How did you know? It's Maria. She's having the baby and it's going badly. Go in quickly. I'll take your horse." He ran across the terrace, unfastened Dr. Fothergill's saddle bags and brought them to him. "Hurry, doctor," he said. "The room to the left. Hurry, for God's sake!"

"Keep calm, young man," said Dr. Fothergill. "I very much doubt if it is going badly. Look after my horse. He's a good horse." As he passed into the house he heard a church clock striking in the distance. Midnight. It was no longer Christmas Eve. It was Christmas Day.

4

At the first cockcrow, that moment of mystery when all living creatures are said to wake and stir, and turn again to their rest, but only the cocks give utterance, the boy was born. He was small but quite sturdy, for all he had been in such a hurry to be a Christmas baby. When he and his mother were sleeping, with Martin to watch over them, Dr. Fothergill went to the kitchen to wash his hands and spruce himself up before riding home to bring the good news of a grandson to Maria's parents. Mrs. Appledore, the midwife whom Martin had brought back from the village, came with him that they might discuss together the excellent termination of what at one point had very nearly been a difficult confinement.

"You came just in time, sir, I do believe," said Mrs. Appledore.

"You would have done it alone, my dear," said Dr. Fothergill.

"I'm not sure, sir. The young gentleman, poor lad, was no help to me. The young lady, she helped herself. She seemed never afraid."

"She's a plucky girl, though devilish headstrong," said Dr. Fothergill. "Who owns this house? Nothing in it but a few rags and sticks of furniture, yet it feels lived in."

"The owner is in foreign parts, sir," said Mrs. Appledore. "He's a queer gentleman. When his brother died and the house came to him he sold all the valuable furniture, and left the rest. He let the stables to a farmer nearby but he's never let the house. Means to live here one day, I'm told."

They moved out into the hall. There was a window beside the front door and through it came flooding the first light of Christmas Day. A west wind from the sea had carried the mist away and one great planet still burned in a clear green sky. Beneath the window the wooded ground fell sharply away to the glory of the moor. For a moment Dr. Fothergill stood at the window for though he knew the moor so well he could never see it unexpectedly like this without profound awe. As he turned back from the window again he saw a portrait hanging on the panelling close to the window. It was of a middle-aged man with powdered hair tied back in a queue. He had straight shoulders and a face of great integrity. Dr. Fothergill looked at it for some time, much moved by it. "Who's that?" he asked. "The owner?"

"Not the present owner, sir. His brother who died."

"How long ago did he die?"

"Ten years ago, sir." Suddenly Mrs. Appledore became garrulous. "He and his lady lived here for many years. They loved the place. They lived here with an old Negro servant. Very attached to them, he was. They had no children and it was a grief to them. Then suddenly my lady she found she was to have a child. She was so happy, and her husband and the old servant too. They were like children, they were so happy. But she died, sir, and the child as well. Her husband and the old servant were heartbroken. They shut up the house and went to foreign parts but after a few months they both caught a fever and died there. I was glad when I heard it. No one couldn't have wanted them to live without my lady."

It seemed a sad story but it was not a sad house. Dr. Fothergill thought he had seldom been in a happier. He opened the parlour door softly to have a last look at his patient, then beckoned to Mrs. Appledore to come and see.

She had brought blankets up from the village with her and Maria lay on a pile of them before the fire. She was asleep, her baby cuddled against her. Martin had stretched himself out on the floor beside her and he, too, was asleep. Utterly relaxed in the deep dreamless sleep of relief and exhaustion they looked much younger than their years. They looked a boy and girl. They had turned a little towards each other in their sleep, the child between them, and Martin had one arm stretched out protectingly over his wife and son.

The two elderly people tiptoed away again and out into the hall. With the door shut Dr. Fothergill blew his nose loudly. He could never get used to it. He had long ago lost count of the number of babies he had brought into the world, yet still the miracle of it seemed new and fresh. He went out and stood on the terrace, and it was the second cockcrow. In the still crystal-clear air he could hear the small trumpets sounding in all directions. Then the fanfare was silent, there was a moment's pause, and the Christmas bells began to ring. A child was born.

5

A month later Dr. Fothergill was called to the bedside of a sick man. He was a scoundrel whom authority had been after for some while and he had been caught at last red-handed; robbery with violence, and Dr. Fothergill was to patch him up to be hanged after the next session. But to his relief he found the man dying. It would be a matter of an hour or less and there was nothing he could do but keep the poor fellow company. He was a hard-bitten criminal type but he was a man, and the mystery of death had always stirred Dr. Fothergill's deep compassion only a little less than the miracle of birth. He sat with his hand lightly on the man's wrist, and he asked him his name and was told it was Tom Badger. He repeated the name quietly, with emphasis, as though he liked it. He believed it gave the dying a sense of their own value, a sense of being cared for as an individual, to say the name like that. Especially a fellow like this scoundrel, for whom probably no one had ever cared at all.

The man was silent for a while and then he said, "You're lucky, doctor."

"Lucky?" asked Dr. Fothergill.

"You nearly had my knife in your back on Christmas Eve."

Dr. Fothergill answered pleasantly, "How was that, Tom?"

"Do you call to mind the boy who brought you a message from Longbarton Farm? I bribed him to give it. I was after your watch and rings, and the money in your pockets. I was desperate that night." His voice died away and Dr. Fothergill waited. Presently he went on, as though he were anxious to get his story told with the last strength that he had. "I missed you going up, the mist was that thick. Coming down I thought I couldn't fail. I was in the bushes just below where the way forks. I was almost as near to you as I am now. I'd have let you pass me and then sprung at you."

"What stopped you, Tom?"

"You turned off right and I was afraid to come after you. I daren't do it. Not with the two of you."

Dr. Fothergill said, "I was alone, Tom."

"No, sir. There was another horseman wheeled in alongside of you."

Dr. Fothergill remained sitting quietly relaxed in his chair but for just a moment the wretched little room seemed to sway about him. Then it steadied and he said, "What did he look like, Tom?"

"A straight back, he had. Grey hair tied with a ribbon. I see his face as clear as though the moon shone on it; though that's queer when you call to mind how thick the mist was. But I see his face clear and I was afeared of him."

Dr. Fothergill had to bend over to catch the last words, and the man seemed to be going, but a few minutes later he opened his eyes again and said clearly, "So you'd best leave me, doctor. You'd have had my knife in your back if I hadn't been afeared."

Dr. Fothergill understood his meaning. He did not wish in his dying moments to claim a sympathy to which he had no right.

Deep in his soul, at the last, there had come a moment of truth.

The doctor's hand tightened a little on his wrist. "I'll not leave you, Tom," he said.

The Sad Shepherd
Henry van Dyke

Darkness

Out of the Valley of Gardens, where a film of new-fallen snow lay smooth as feathers on the breast of a dove, the ancient Pools of Solomon looked up into the night sky with dark, tranquil eyes, wide-open and passive, reflecting the crisp stars and the small, round moon. The full springs, overflowing on the hill-side, melted their way through the field of white in winding channels, and along their course the grass was green even in the dead of winter.

But the sad shepherd walked far above the friendly valley, in a region where ridges of gray rock welted and scarred the back of the earth, like wounds of half-forgotten strife and battles long ago. The solitude was forbidding and disquieting; the keen air that searched the wanderer had no pity in it; and the myriad glances of the night were curiously cold.

His flock straggled after him. The sheep, weather beaten and dejected, followed the path with low heads nodding from side to side, as if they had travelled far and found little pasture. The black, lop-eared goats leaped upon the rocks, restless and ravenous, tearing down the tender branches and leaves of the dwarf oaks and wild olives. They reared up against the twisted trunks and crawled and scrambled among the boughs. It was like a company of gray downcast friends and a troop of merry little black devils following the sad shepherd afar off.

He walked looking on the ground, paying small heed to them. Now and again, when the sound of pattering feet and panting breath and the rustling and rending among the copses fell too far behind, he drew out his shepherd's pipe and blew a strain of music, shrill and mournful, quavering and lamenting through the hollow night. He waited while the troops of gray and black scuffed and bounded and trotted near to him. Then he dropped the pipe into its place again and strode forward, looking on the ground.

The fitful, shivery wind that rasped the hill-top fluttered the rags of his long mantle of Tyrian blue, torn by thorns and stained by travel. The rich tunic of striped silk beneath it was worn thin, and the girdle about his loins had lost all its ornaments of silver and jewels. His curling hair hung down dishevelled under a turban of fine linen, in which the gilt threads were frayed and tarnished; and his shoes of soft leather were broken by the road. On his brown fingers the places of the vanished rings were still marked in white skin. He carried not the long staff nor the heavy nail-studded rod of the shepherd, but a slender stick of carved cedar battered and scratched by hard usage, and the handle, which must once have been of precious metal, was missing.

He was a strange figure for that lonely place and that humble occupation—a branch of faded beauty from some royal garden tossed by rude winds into the wilderness—a pleasure craft adrift, buffeted and broken, on rough seas.

But he seemed to have passed beyond caring. His young face was as frayed and threadbare as his garments. The splendour of the moonlight flooding the wide world meant as little to him as the hardness of the rugged track which he followed. He wrapped his tattered mantle closer to him, and strode ahead, looking on the ground.

As the path dropped from the summit of the ridge toward the Valley of Mills and passed among huge broken rocks, three men sprang at him from the shadows. He lifted his stick, but let it fall again, and a strange ghost of a smile twisted his face as they gripped him and threw him down.

"You are rough beggars," he said. "Say what you want, you are welcome to it."

"Your money, dog of a courtier," they muttered fiercely. "Give us your golden collar, Herod's hound, quick, or you die!"

"The quicker, the better," he answered, closing his eyes.

The bewildered flock of sheep and goats, gathered in a silent ring, stood at gaze while the robbers fumbled over their master.

"This is a stray dog," said one. "He has lost his collar, there is not even the price of a mouthful of wine on him. Shall we kill him and leave him for the vultures?"

"What have the vultures done for us," said another, "that we should feed them? Let us take his cloak and drive off his flock, and leave him to die in his own time."

With a kick and a curse they left him. He opened his eyes and lay quiet for a moment, with his twisted smile, watching the stars.

"You creep like snails," he said. "I thought you had marked my time to-night. But not even that is given to me for nothing. I must pay for all, it seems."

Far away, slowly scattering and receding, he heard the rustling and bleating of his frightened flock as the robbers, running and shouting, tried to drive them over the hills. Then he stood up and took the shepherd's pipe from the breast of his tunic. He blew again that sad, piercing air, sounding it out over the ridges and distant thickets. It seemed to have neither beginning nor end; a melancholy, pleading tune that searched forever after something lost.

While he played, the sheep and the goats, slipping away from their captors by roundabout ways, hiding behind the laurel bushes, following the dark gullies, leaping down the broken cliffs, came circling back to him, one after another; and as they came, he interrupted his playing, now and then, to call them by name.

When they were nearly all assembled, he went down swiftly toward the lower valley, and they followed him, panting. At the last crook of the path on the steep hillside a straggler came after him along the cliff. He looked up and saw it outlined against the sky. Then he saw it leap, and slip, and fall beyond the path into a deep cleft.

"Little fool," he said, "fortune is kind to you! You have escaped from the big trap of life. What? You are crying for help? You are still in the trap? Then I must go down to you, little fool, for I am

a fool too. But why I must do it, I know no more than you know."

He lowered himself quickly and perilously into the cleft, and found the creature with its leg broken and bleeding. It was not a sheep, but a young goat. He had no cloak to wrap it in, but he took off his turban and unrolled it, and bound it around the trembling animal. Then he climbed back to the path and strode on at the head of his flock, carrying the little black kid in his arms.

There were houses in the Valley of the Mills; and in some of them lights were burning; and the drone of the mill-stones, where the women were still grinding, came out into the night like the humming of drowsy bees. As the women heard the pattering and bleating of the flock, they wondered who was passing so late. One of them, in a house where there was no mill but many lights, came to the door and looked out laughing, her face and bosom bare.

But the sad shepherd did not stay. His long shadow and the confused mass of lesser shadows behind him drifted down the white moonlight, past the yellow bars of lamplight that gleamed from the doorways. It seemed as if he were bound to go somewhere and would not delay.

Yet with all his haste to be gone, it was plain that he thought little of where he was going. For when he came to the foot of the valley, where the paths divided, he stood between them staring vacantly, without a desire to turn him this way or that. The imperative of choice halted him like a barrier. The balance of his mind hung even because both scales were empty. He could act, he could go, for his strength was untouched; but he could not choose, for his will was broken within him.

The path to the left went up toward the little town of Bethlehem, with huddled roofs and walls in silhouette along the double-crested hill. It was dark and forbidding as a closed fortress. The sad shepherd looked at it with indifferent eyes; there was nothing there to draw him.

The path to the right wound through rock-strewn valleys toward the Dead Sea. But rising out of that crumpled wilderness, a mile or two away, the smooth white ribbon of a chariot-road lay upon the flank of a cone-shaped mountain and curled in loops toward its peak. There the great cone was cut squarely off, and the levelled summit was capped by a palace of marble, with round towers at the corners and flaring beacons along the walls; and the glow of an immense fire, hidden in the central courtyard, painted a false dawn in the eastern sky. All down the clean-cut mountain slopes, on terraces and blind arcades, the lights flashed from lesser pavilions and pleasure-houses.

It was the secret orchard of Herod and his friends, their trysting-place with the spirits of mirth and madness. They called it the Mountain of the Little Paradise. Rich gardens were there; and the cool water from the Pools of Solomon splashed in the fountains; and trees of the knowledge of good and evil fruited blood-red and ivory-white above them; and smooth, curving, glistening shapes, whispering softly of pleasures, lay among the flowers and glided behind the trees. All this was now hidden in the dark. Only the strange bulk of the mountain, a sharp black pyramid girdled and crowded with fire, loomed across the night—a mountain once seen never to be forgotten.

The sad shepherd remembered it well. He looked at it with the eyes of a child who had been in hell. It burned him from afar. Turning neither to the right nor to the left, he walked without a path straight out upon the plain of Bethlehem, still whitened in the hollows and on the sheltered side of its rounded hillocks by the veil of snow.

He faced a wide and empty world. To the west in sleeping Bethlehem, to the east in flaring Herodium, the life of man was infinitely far away from him. Even the stars seemed to withdraw themselves against the blue-black of the sky. They diminished and receded till they were like pinholes in the vault above him. The moon in mid-heaven shrank into a bit of burnished silver, hard and glittering, immeasurably remote. The ragged, inhospitable ridges of Tekoa lay stretched in mortal slumber along the horizon, and between them he caught a glimpse of the sunken Lake of Death, darkly gleaming in its deep bed. There was no movement, no sound, on the plain where he walked, except the soft-padding feet of his dumb, obedient flock.

He felt an endless isolation strike cold to his heart, against which he held the limp body of the wounded kid, wondering the while, with a half-contempt for his own foolishness, why he took such trouble to save a tiny scrap of the worthless tissue which is called life.

Even when a man does not know or care where he is going, if he steps onward he will get there. In an hour or more of walking over the plain, the sad shepherd came to a sheep-fold of grey stones with a rude tower beside it. The fold was full of sheep, and at the foot of the tower a little fire of thorns was burning, around which four shepherds were crouching, wrapped in their thick woolen cloaks.

As the stranger approached them they looked up, and one of them rose quickly to his feet, grasping his knotted club. But when they saw the flock that followed the sad shepherd, they stared at each other and said: "It is one of us, a keeper of sheep. But how comes he here in this raiment? It is what men wear in kings' houses."

"No," said the one who was standing. "It is what they wear when they have been thrown out of them. Look at the rags. He may be a thief and robber with his stolen flock."

"Salute him when he comes near," said the oldest shepherd. "Are we not four to one? We have nothing to fear from a ragged traveller. Speak him fair. It is the will of God—and it costs nothing."

"Peace be with you, brother," cried the youngest shepherd. "May your mother and father be blessed."

"May your heart be enlarged," the stranger answered, "and may all your families be more blessed than mine, for I have none."

"A homeless man," said the old shepherd, "has either been robbed by his fellows, or punished by God."

"I do not know which it was," answered the stranger. "The end is the same, as you see."

"By your speech you come from Galilee. Where are you going? What are you seeking here?"

"I was going nowhere, my masters; but it was cold on the way there, and my feet turned to your fire."

"Come then, if you are a peaceable man, and warm your feet with us. Heat is a good gift; divide it and it is not less. But you shall have bread and salt too, if you will."

"May your hospitality enrich you. I am your unworthy servant. But my flock?"

"Let your flock shelter by the south wall of the fold; there is good picking there and no wind. Come you and sit with us."

So they all sat down by the fire; and the sad shepherd ate of their bread, but sparingly, like a man to whom hunger brings a need but no joy in the satisfying of it; and the others were silent for a proper time, out of courtesy. Then the oldest shepherd spoke: "My name is Zadok the son of Eliezer, of Bethlehem. I am the chief shepherd of the flocks of the Temple, which are before you in the fold. These are my sister's sons, Jotham and Shama, and Nathan: their father Elkanah is dead; and but for these I am a childless man."

"My name," replied the stranger, "is Ammiel the son of Jochanan, of the city of Bethsaida, by the Sea of Galilee, and I am a fatherless man."

"It is better to be childless than fatherless," said Zadok, "yet it is the will of God that children should bury their fathers. When did the blessed Jochanan die?"

"I know not whether he be dead or alive. It is three years since I looked upon his face or had word of him."

"You are an exile, then? He has cast you off?"

"It was the other way," said Ammiel, looking on the ground.

At this the shepherd Shama, who had listened with doubt in his face, started up in anger. "Pig of a Galilean," he cried, "despiser of parents! Breaker of the law! When I saw you coming I knew you for something vile. Why do you darken the night for us with your presence? You have reviled him who begot you. Away, or we stone you!"

Ammiel did not answer or move. The twisted smile passed over his face again as he waited to know the shepherd's will with him, even as he had waited for the robbers. But Zadok lifted his hand.

"Not so hasty, Shama-ben-Elkanah. You also break the law by judging a man unheard. The rabbis have told us that there is a tradition of the elders—a rule as holy as the law itself—that a man may deny his father in a certain way without sin. It is a strange rule, and it must be very holy or it would not be so strange. But this is the teaching of the elders: a son may say of anything for

107

which his father asks him—a sheep, or a measure of corn, or a field, or a purse of silver—'it is Corban, a gift that I have vowed unto the Lord'; and so his father shall have no more claim upon him. Have you said 'Corban' to your father, Ammiel-ben-Jochanan? Have you made a vow unto the Lord?"

"I have said 'Corban'," answered Ammiel, lifting his face, still shadowed by that strange smile, "but it was not the Lord who heard my vow."

"Tell us what you have done," said the old man sternly, "for we will neither judge you, nor shelter you, unless we hear your story."

"There is nothing in it," replied Ammiel indifferently. "It is an old story. But if you are curious you shall hear it. Afterward you shall deal with me as you will."

So the shepherds, wrapped in their warm cloaks, sat listening with grave faces and watchful, unsearchable eyes, while Ammiel in his tattered silk sat by the sinking fire of thorns and told his tale with a voice that had no room for hope or fear—a cool, dead voice that spoke only of things ended.

Nightfire

"In my father's house I was the second son. My brother was honored and trusted in all things. He was a prudent man and profitable to the household. All that he counselled was done, all that he wished he had. My place was a narrow one. There was neither honor nor joy in it, for it was filled with daily tasks and rebukes. No one cared for me. My mother sometimes wept when I was rebuked. Perhaps she was disappointed in me. But she had no power to make things better. I felt that I was a beast of burden, fed only in order that I might be useful; and the dull life irked me like an ill-fitting harness. There was nothing in it.

"I went to my father and claimed my share of the inheritance. He was rich. He gave it to me. It did not impoverish him and it made me free. I said to him 'Corban' and shook the dust of Bethsaida from my feet.

"I went out to look for mirth and love and joy and all that is pleasant to the eyes and sweet to the taste. If a god made me, thought I, he made me to live, and the pride of life was strong in my heart and in my flesh. My vow was offered to that well-known god. I served him in Jerusalem, in Alexandria, in Rome, for his altars are everywhere and men worship him openly or in secret.

"My money and youth made me welcome to his followers, and I spent them both freely as if they could never come to an end. I clothed myself in purple and fine linen and fared sumptuously every day. The wine of Cyprus and the dishes of Egypt and Syria were on my table. My dwelling was crowded with merry guests. They came for what I gave them. Their faces were hungry and their soft touch was like the clinging of leeches. To them I was nothing but money and youth; no longer a beast of burden—a beast of pleasure. There was nothing in it.

"From the richest fare my heart went away empty, and after the wildest banquet my soul fell drunk and solitary into sleep.

"Then I thought, power is better than pleasure. If a man will feast and revel, let him do it with the great. They will favour him and raise him up for the services he renders them. He will obtain place and authority in the world and gain many friends. So I joined myself with Herod."

When the sad shepherd spoke this name his listeners drew back from him as if it were a defilement to hear it. They spat upon the ground and cursed the Idumean who called himself their king.

"A slave!" Jotham cried, "A bloody tyrant and a slave from Edom! A fox, a vile beast who devours his own children! God burn him in Gehenna!"

The old Zadok picked up a stone and threw it into the darkness, saying slowly, "I cast this stone on the grave of the Idumean, the blasphemer, the defiler of the Temple! God send us soon the Deliverer, the Promised One, the true King of Israel!" Ammiel made no sign, but went on with his story.

"Herod used me well—for his own purpose. He welcomed me to his palace and his table, and gave me a place among his favorites. He was so much my friend that he borrowed my money. There were many of the nobles of Jerusalem with him, Sadducees, and proselytes from Rome and Asia, and women from everywhere. The law of Israel was observed in the open court, when the people were watching. But in the secret feasts there was no law but the will of Herod, and many deities were served but no god was worshipped. There the captains and the princes of Rome consorted with the high-priest and his sons by night; and there was much coming and going by hidden ways. Everybody was a borrower or a seller of favors. It was a house of diligent madness. There was nothing in it.

"In the midst of this whirling life a great need of love came upon me and I wished to love someone in my inmost heart.

"At a certain place in the city, within closed doors, I saw a young slave-girl dancing. She was about fifteen years old, thin and supple; she danced like a reed in the wind; but her eyes were weary as death, and her white body was marked with bruises. She stumbled and the men laughed at her. She fell and her mistress beat her, crying out that she would fain be rid of such a heavy-footed slave. I paid the price and took her to my dwelling.

"Her name was Tamar. She was a daughter of Lebanon. I robed her in silk and broidered linen. I nourished her with tender care so that beauty came upon her like the blossoming of an almond tree; she was a garden enclosed, breathing spices. Her eyes were like doves behind her veil, her lips were a thread of scarlet, her neck was a tower of ivory, and her breasts were as two fawns which feed among the lilies. She was whiter than milk, and more rosy than the flower of the peach, and her dancing was like the flight of a bird among the branches. So I loved her.

"She lay in my bosom as a clear stone that one has bought and polished and set in fine gold at the end of a golden chain. Never was she glad at my coming, or sorry at my going. Never did she give me anything except what I took from her. There was nothing in it.

"Now whether Herod knew of the jewel I kept in my dwelling I cannot tell. It was sure that he had his spies in all the city, and himself walked the streets by night in a disguise. On a certain day he sent for me, and had me into his secret chamber, professing great love toward me and more confidence than in any man that lived. So I must go to Rome for him, bearing a sealed letter and a private message for Caesar. All my goods would be left safely in the hands of the king, my friend, who would reward me double. There was a certain place of high authority at Jerusalem which Caesar would gladly bestow on a Jew who had done him a service. This mission would commend me to him. It was a great occasion, suited to my powers. Thus Herod fed me with fair promises, and I ran his errand. There was nothing in it.

"I stood before Caesar and gave him the letter. He read it and laughed, saying that a prince with an incurable hunger is a servant of value to an emperor. Then he asked me if there was nothing sent with the letter. I answered that there was no gift, but a message for his private ear. He drew me aside and I told him that Herod begged earnestly that his dear son, Antipater, might be sent back in haste from Rome to Palestine, for the king had great need of him.

"At this, Caesar laughed again. 'To bury him, I suppose,' he said, 'with his brothers, Alexander and Aristobulus! Truly, it is better to be Herod's swine than his son! Tell the old fox that he may catch his own prey.' With that he turned from me and I withdrew unrewarded, to make my way back, as best I could with an empty purse, to Palestine. I had seen the Lord of the World. There was nothing in it.

"Selling my rings and bracelets I got passage in a trading ship for Joppa. There I heard that the king was not in Jerusalem, at his Palace of the Upper City, but had gone with his friends to make merry for a month on the Mountain of Little Paradise. On that hill-top over against us, where the lights are flaring to-night, in the banquet-hall where couches are spread for a hundred guests, I found Herod."

The listening shepherds spat upon the ground again, and Jotham muttered, "May the worms that devour his flesh never die!" But Zadok whispered, "We wait for the Lord's salvation to come out of Zion." And the sad shepherd, looking with fixed eyes at the firelit mountain far away, continued his story:

"The king lay on his ivory couch, and the sweat of his disease was heavy upon him, for he was old, and his flesh was corrupted. But his hair and his beard were dyed and perfumed and there was a wreath of roses on his head. The hall was full of nobles and great men, the sons of the high-priest were there, and the servants poured their wine in cups of gold. There was a sound of soft music; and all the men were watching a girl who danced in the middle of the hall; and the eyes of Herod were fiery, like the eyes of a fox.

"The dancer was Tamar. She glistened like the snow on Lebanon, and the redness of her was ruddier than a pomegranate, and her dancing was like the coiling of white serpents. When the dance was ended her attendants threw a veil of gauze over her and she lay among her cushions, half covered with flowers, at the feet of the king.

"Through the sound of clapping hands and shouting, two slaves led me behind the couch of Herod. His eyes narrowed as they fell upon me. I told him the message of Caesar, making it soft, as if it were a word that suffered him to catch his prey. He stroked his beard and his look fell on Tamar. 'I have caught it,' he murmured; 'by all the gods, I have always caught it. And my dear son Antipater is coming home of his own free will. I have lured him, he is mine.'

"Then a look of madness crossed his face and he sprang up, with frothing lips, and struck at me. 'What is this,' he cried, 'a spy, a servant of my false son, a traitor in my banquet-hall! Who are you?' I knelt before him, protesting that he must know me; that I was his friend, his messenger; that I had left all my goods in his hands; that the girl who had danced for him was mine. At this his face changed again and he fell back on his couch, shaken with horrible laughter. 'Yours!' he cried. 'When was she yours? What is yours? I know you now, poor madman. You are Ammiel, a crazy shepherd from Galilee, who troubled us some time since. Take him away, slaves. He has twenty sheep and twenty goats among my flock at the foot of the mountain. See to it that he gets them, and drive him away.'

"I fought against the slaves with my bare hands, but they held me. I called to Tamar, begging her to have pity on me, to speak for me, to come with me. She looked up with her eyes like doves behind her veil, but there was no knowledge of me in them. She laughed lazily, as if it were a poor comedy, and flung a broken rose-branch in my face. Then the silver cord was loosened within me, and my heart went out, and I struggled no more. There was nothing in it.

"Afterward I found myself on the road with this flock. I led them past Hebron into the south country, and so by the Vale of Eshcol, and over many hills beyond the Pools of Solomon, until my feet brought me to your fire. Here I rest on the way to nowhere."

He sat silent, and the four shepherds looked at him with amazement.

"It is a bitter tale," said Shama, "and you are a great sinner."

"I should be a fool not to know that," answered the sad shepherd, "but the knowledge does me no good."

"You must repent," said Nathan, the youngest shepherd, in a friendly voice.

"How can a man repent," answered the sad shepherd, "unless he has hope? But I am sorry for everything, and most of all for living."

"Would you not live to kill the fox Herod?" cried Jotham fiercely.

"Why should I let him out of the trap?" answered the sad shepherd. "Is he not dying more slowly than I could kill him?"

"You must have faith in God," said Zadok earnestly and gravely.

"He is too far away."

"Then you must have love for your neighbour."

"He is too near. My confidence in man was like a pool by the wayside. It was shallow, but there was water in it, and sometimes a star shone there. Now the feet of many beasts have trampled through it, and the jackals have drunken of it, and there is no more water. It is dry and the mire is caked at the bottom."

"Is there nothing good in the world?"

"There is pleasure, but I am sick of it. There is power, but I hate it. There is wisdom, but I mistrust it. Life is a game and every player is for his own hand. Mine is played. I have nothing to win or lose."

"You are young; you have many years to live."

"I am old, yet the days before me are too many."

"But you travel the road, you go forward. Do you hope for nothing?"

"I hope for nothing," said the sad shepherd. "Yet if one thing should come to me, it might be the beginning of hope. If I saw in man or woman a deed of kindness without a selfish reason, and a

proof of love gladly given for its own sake only, then might I turn my face toward that light. Till that comes, how can I have faith in God whom I have never seen? I have seen the world which he has made, and it brings me no faith. There is nothing in it."

"Ammiel-ben-Jochanan," said the old man sternly, "you are a son of Israel, and we have had compassion on you, according to the law. But you are an apostate, an unbeliever, and we can have no more fellowship with you, lest a curse come upon us. The company of the desperate brings misfortune. Go your way and depart from us, for our way is not yours."

So the sad shepherd thanked them for their entertainment, and took the little kid again in his arms, and went into the night, calling his flock. But the youngest shepherd Nathan followed him a few steps and said, "There is a broken fold at the foot of the hill. It is old and small, but you may find a shelter there for your flock where the wind will not shake you. Go your way with God, brother, and see better days."

Then Ammiel went a little way down the hill and sheltered his flock in a corner of the crumbling walls. He lay among the sheep and the goats with his face upon his folded arms, and whether the time passed slowly or swiftly he did not know, for he slept.

He waked as Nathan came running and stumbling among the scattered stone.

"We have seen a vision," he cried, "a wonderful vision of angels. Did you not hear them? They sang loudly of the Hope of Israel. We are going to Bethlehem to see this thing which is come to pass. Come you and keep watch over our sheep while we are gone."

"Of angels I have seen and heard nothing," said Ammiel, "but I will guard your flocks with mine, since I am in debt to you for your bread and fire."

So he brought the kid in his arms, and the weary flock straggling after him, to the south wall of the great fold again, and sat there by embers at the foot of the tower, while the others were away.

The moon rested like a ball on the edge of the western hills and rolled behind them. The stars faded in the east and the fires went out on the Mountain of the Little Paradise. Over the hills of Moab,

a gray flood of dawn rose slowly, and arrows of red shot far up before the sunrise.

The shepherds returned full of joy and told what they had seen.

"It was even as the angels said unto us," said Shama, "and it must be true. The King of Israel has come. The faithful shall be blessed."

"Herod shall fall," cried Jotham, lifting his clenched fist toward the dark mountain. "Burn, black Idumean, in the bottomless pit, where the fire is not quenched."

Zadok spoke more quietly. "We found the new-born child of whom the angels told us wrapped in swaddling clothes and lying in a manger. The ways of God are wonderful. His salvation comes out of darkness. But you, Ammiel-ben-Jochanan, except you believe, you shall not see it. Yet since you have kept our flocks faithfully, and because of the joy that has come to us, I give you this piece of silver to help you on your way."

But Nathan came close to the sad shepherd and touched him on the shoulder with a friendly hand. "Go you also to Bethlehem," he said in a low voice, "for it is good to see what we have seen, and we will keep your flock until you return."

"I will go," said Ammiel, looking into his face, "for I think you wish me well. But whether I shall see what you have seen, or whether I shall ever return, I know not. Farewell."

Dawn

The narrow streets of Bethlehem were waking to the first stir of life as the sad shepherd came into the town with the morning, and passed through them like one walking in his sleep.

The courtyard of the great inn and the open rooms around it were crowded with travellers, rousing from their night's rest and making ready for the day's journey. In front of the stables half hollowed in the rock beside the inn, men were saddling their horses and their beasts of burden, and there was much noise and confusion.

But beyond these, at the end of the line, there was a deeper grotto in the rock, which was used only when the nearer stalls were full. Beside the entrance of this cave, an ass was tethered, and a man of middle age stood in the doorway.

The sad shepherd saluted him and told his name.

"I am Joseph the carpenter of Nazareth," replied the man. "Have you also seen the angels of whom your brother shepherds came to tell us?"

"I have seen no angels," answered Ammiel, "nor have I any brothers among the shepherds. But I would fain see what they have seen."

"It is our first-born son," said Joseph, "and the Most High has sent him to us. He is a marvellous child; great things are foretold of him. You may go in, but quietly, for the child and his mother Mary are asleep."

So the sad shepherd went in quietly. His long shadow entered before him, for the sunrise was flowing into the door of the grotto. It was clean and put in order, and a bed of straw was laid in the corner on the ground.

The child was asleep, but the young mother was waking, for she had taken him from the manger into her lap, where her maiden veil of white was spread to receive him. And she was singing very softly as she bent over him in wonder and content.

Ammiel saluted her and kneeled down to look at the child. He saw nothing different from other young children. The mother waited for him to speak of angels, as the other shepherds had done. The sad shepherd did not speak, but only looked. And as he looked, his face changed.

"You have suffered pain and danger and sorrow for his sake," he said gently.

"They are past," she answered, "and for his sake I have suffered them gladly."

"He is very little and helpless; you must bear many troubles for his sake."

"To care for him is my joy, and to bear him lightens my burden."

"He does not know you; he can do nothing for you."

"But I know him. I have carried him under my heart. He is my son and my king."

"Why do you love him?"

The mother looked up at the sad shepherd with a great reproach in her soft eyes. Then her look grew pitiful as it rested on his face.

"You are a sorrowful man," she said.

"I am a wicked man," he answered.

She shook her head gently.

"I know nothing of that," she said, "but you must be very sorrowful, since you are born of a woman and yet you ask a mother why she loves her child. I love him for love's sake, because God has given him to me."

So the mother Mary leaned over her little son again and began to croon a song as if she were alone with him.

But Ammiel was still there, watching and thinking and beginning to remember. It came back to him that there was a woman in Galilee who had wept when he was rebuked; whose eyes had followed him when he was unhappy, as if she longed to do something for him; whose voice had broken and dropped silent while she covered her tear-stained face when he went away.

His thoughts flowed swiftly and silently toward her and after her like rapid waves of light. There was a thought of her bending over a little child in her lap, singing softly for pure joy—and the child was himself. There was a thought of her lifting a little child to the breast that had borne him as a burden and a pain, to nourish him there as a comfort and a treasure—and the child was himself. There was a thought of her watching and tending and guiding a little child from day to day, from year to year, putting tender arms around him, bending over his first wavering steps, rejoicing in his joys, wiping away the tears from his eyes, as he had never tried to wipe her tears away—and the child was himself. She had done everything for the child's sake, but what had the child done for her sake? And the child was himself; that was what he had come to—after the nightfire had burned out, after the darkness had grown thin and melted in the thoughts that pulsed through it like rapid waves of light—that was what he had come to in the early morning—himself, a child in his mother's arms.

Then he arose and went out of the grotto softly, making the three-fold sign of reverence; and the eyes of Mary followed him with kind looks.

Joseph of Nazareth was still waiting outside the door.

"How was it that you did not see the angels?" he asked. "Were you not with the other shepherds?"

"No," answered Ammiel, "I was asleep. But I have seen the mother and the child. Blessed be the house that holds them."

"You are strangely clad for a shepherd," said Joseph. "Where do you come from?"

"From a far country," said Ammiel. "From a country that you have never visited."

"Where are you going now?" asked Joseph.

"I am going home," answered Ammiel, "to my mother's and my father's house in Galilee."

"Go in peace, friend," said Joseph.

And the sad shepherd took up his battered staff, and went on his way rejoicing.

The Sin of the Prince Bishop

William Canton

he Prince Bishop Evrard stood gazing at his marvellous Cathedral; and as he let his eyes wander in delight over the three deep sculptured portals and the double gallery above them, and the great rose window, and the ringers' gallery, and so up to the massive western towers, he felt as though his heart were clapping hands for joy within him. And he thought to himself, "Surely in all the world God has no more beautiful house than this which I have built with such long labor and at so princely an outlay of my treasure." And thus the Prince Bishop fell into the sin of vainglory, and, though he was a holy man, he did not perceive that he had fallen, so filled with gladness was he at the sight of his completed work.

In the double gallery of the west front there were many great statues with crowns and sceptres, but a niche over the central portal was empty, and this the Prince Bishop intended to fill with a statue of himself. It was to be a very small simple statue, as became one who prized lowliness of heart, but as he looked up at the vacant place it gave him pleasure to think that hundreds of years after he was dead people would pause before his effigy and praise him and his work. And this, too, was vainglory.

As the Prince Bishop lay asleep that night a mighty six-winged Angel stood beside him and bade him rise. "Come," he said, "and I will show thee some of those who have worked with thee in building the great church, and whose service in God's eyes has been more worthy than thine." And the Angel led him past the Cathedral and down the steep street of the ancient city, and though it was midday, the people going to and fro did not seem to see them. Beyond the gates they followed the shelving road till they came to green level fields, and there in the middle of the road, between grassy banks covered white with cherry blossom, two great white oxen, yoked to a huge block of stone, stood resting before they began the toilsome ascent.

"Look!" said the Angel; and the Prince Bishop saw a little blue-winged bird which perched on the stout yoke beam fastened to the horns of the oxen, and sang such a heavenly song of rest and contentment that the big shaggy creatures ceased to blow stormily through their nostrils, and drew long tranquil breaths instead.

"Look again!" said the Angel. And from a hut of wattles and clay a little peasant girl came with a bundle of hay in her arms, and gave first one of the oxen and then the other a wisp. Then she stroked their black muzzles, and laid her rosy face against their white cheeks. Then the Prince Bishop saw the rude teamster rise from his rest on the bank and cry to his cattle, and the oxen strained against the beam and the thick ropes tightened, and the huge block of stone was once more set in motion.

And when the Prince Bishop saw that it was these fellow-workers whose service was more worthy in God's eyes than his own, he was abashed and sorrowful for his sin, and the tears of his own weeping awoke him. So he sent for the master of the sculptors and bade him fill the little niche over the middle portal, not with his own effigy but with an image of the child; and he bade him make two colossal figures of the white oxen; and to the great wonderment of the people these were set up high in the tower so that men could see them against the blue sky. "And as for me," he said, "let my body be buried, with my face downward, outside the great church, in front of the middle entrance, that men may trample on my vainglory and that I may serve them as a stepping-stone to the house of God; and the little child shall look on me when I lie in the dust."

Now the little girl in the niche was carved with wisps of hay in her hands, but the child who had fed the oxen knew nothing of this, and as she grew up she forgot her childish service, so that when she had grown to womanhood and chanced to see this statue over the portal she did not know it was her own self in stone. But what she had done was not forgotten in heaven.

And as for the oxen, one of them looked east and one looked west across the wide fruitful country about the foot of the hill-city. And one caught the first grey gleam, and the first rosy flush, and the first golden splendor of the sunrise; and the other was lit with the color of the sunset long after the lowlands had faded away in the blue mist of the twilight. Weary men and worn women looking up at them felt that a gladness and a glory and a deep peace had fallen on the life of toil. And then, when people began to understand, they said it was well that these mighty laborers, who had helped to build the house, should still find a place of service and honor in the house; and they remembered that the Master of the house had once been a Babe warmed in a manger by the breath of kine. And at the thought of this men grew more pitiful to their cattle, and to the beasts in servitude, and to all dumb animals. And that was one good fruit which sprang from the Prince Bishop's repentance.

Now over the colossal stone oxen hung the bells of the Cathedral. On Christmas Eve the ringers, according to the old custom, ascended to their gallery to ring in the birth of the Babe Divine. At the moment of midnight the master ringer gave the word, and the great bells began to swing in joyful sequence. Down below in the crowded church lay the image of the newborn Child on the cold straw, and at His haloed head stood the images of the ox and the ass. Far out across the snow-roofed city, far away over the white glistening country rang the glad music of the tower. People who went to their doors to listen cried in astonishment: "Hark! What strange music is that? It sounds as if the lowing of cattle were mingled with the chimes of the bells." In truth it was so. And in every byre the oxen and the kine answered the strange sweet cadences with their lowing, and the great stone oxen lowed back to their kin of the meadow through the deep notes of the joy-peal.

In the fulness of time the Prince Bishop Evrard died and was buried as he had willed, with his face humbly turned to the earth; and to this day the weather-wasted figure of the little girl looks down on him from her niche, and the slab over his grave serves as a stepping-stone to pious feet.

The Miracle of Love Expressed

Christmas Day in the Morning

Pearl S. Buck

He woke suddenly, and completely. It was four o'clock, the hour at which his father had always called to him to get up and help with the milking. Strange how the habits of his youth clung to him still. Fifty years ago, and his father had been dead for thirty years, and yet he waked at four o'clock in the morning. He had trained himself to turn over and go to sleep, but this morning it was Christmas, he did not try to sleep. Why did he feel so awake tonight? He slipped back in time, as he did so easily nowadays. He was fifteen years old and still at his father's farm. He loved his father. He had not known it until one day a few days before Christmas when he had overheard what his father was saying to his mother.

"Mary, I hate to call Rob in the mornings. He's growing so fast and he needs his sleep. If you could see how he sleeps when I go in to wake him up! I wish I could manage alone." "Well, you can't, Adam." His mother's voice was brisk. "Besides, he isn't a child anymore. It's time he took his turn." "Yes," his father said slowly. "But I sure do hate to wake him."

When he heard these words, something in him woke; his father loved him! He had never thought of it before, taking for granted the tie of their blood. Neither his father nor his mother talked about loving their children—they had no time for such things. There was always so much to do on the farm. Now that he knew his father loved him, there would be no more loitering in the mornings and having to be called again. He got up after that, stumbling blind with sleep, and pulled on his clothes, his eyes tight shut, but he got up.

And then on the night before Christmas, that year when he was fifteen, he lay for a few minutes thinking about the next day. They were poor and most of the excitement was in the turkey they had raised themselves and the mince pies his mother made. His sisters sewed presents and his mother and father always bought something he needed, not only a warm jacket, but maybe something more, such as a book. And he saved and bought them each something, too. He wished, that Christmas he was fifteen, he had a better present for his father. As usual he had gone to the ten-cent store and bought a tie. It had seemed nice enough until he lay thinking the night before Christmas. He looked out of his attic window, the stars were bright.

"Dad," he had once asked when he was a little boy, "What is a stable?" "It's a barn," his father had replied, "like ours." "Then Jesus had been born in a barn, and to a barn the shepherds had come . . ." The thought struck him like a silver dagger. Why should he not give his father a special gift too, out there in the barn? He could get up early, earlier than four, and he could creep into the barn and get all the milking done. He'd do it alone, milk and clean up, and then when his father went to start the milking, he'd see it all done. And he would know who had done it. He laughed to himself as he gazed at the stars. It was what he would do, and he mustn't sleep too sound.

He must have waked twenty times, scratching a match each time to look at his old watch—midnight, and half past one, and then two o'clock. At a quarter to three he got up and put on his clothes. He crept downstairs, careful of the creaky boards, and let himself out. The cows looked at him, sleepy and surprised. It was too early for them too. He had never milked all alone before, but it seemed almost easy. He kept thinking about his father's surprise. His father would come in and get him, saying he would get things started while Rob was getting dressed. He'd go to the barn, open the door, and then he'd go to get the two empty milk cans. But they wouldn't be waiting or empty; they'd be standing in the milk house, filled. He smiled and milked steadily, two strong streams rushing into the pail, frothing and fragrant. The task went more easily than he had ever known it to go before. Milking for once was not a chore. It was something else, a gift to his father, who loved him. He finished, the two milk cans were full, and he covered them and closed them and closed the milk house door carefully.

Back in his room he had only a minute to pull off his clothes in the darkness and jump into bed, for he heard his father up. He put the covers over his head to silence his quick breathing. The door opened.

"Rob!" his father called. "We have to get up, son, even if it is Christmas."

"Aw-right," he said sleepily. The door closed and he lay still, laughing to himself. In just a few minutes his father would know. His dancing heart was ready to jump from his body. The minutes were endless—ten, fifteen, he did not know how many—and he heard his father's footsteps again. The door opened and he lay still.

"Rob!"

"Yes, Dad." His father was laughing, a queer, sobbing sort of laugh. "Thought you'd fool me, did you?" His father was standing beside his bed, feeling for him, pulling away the cover. "It's for Christmas, Dad!"

He found his father and clutched him in a great hug. He felt his father's arms go around him. It was dark and they could not see each other's faces. "Rob, I thank you. Nobody ever did a nicer thing!"

"Oh, Dad, I want you to know, I do want to be good!" The words broke from him on their own will. He did not know what to say. His heart was bursting with love. He got up and pulled on his clothes again and they went down to the Christmas tree. Oh, what a Christmas, and how his heart had nearly burst again with shyness and pride as his father told his mother and made the three younger children listen how he, Rob, had got up all by himself.

"The best Christmas gift I ever had, and I'll remember it, son, every year on Christmas morning, so long as I live." They had both remembered it, and now that his father was dead, he remembered it alone; that blessed Christmas dawn when, alone with the cows in the barn, he had made his first gift of true love.

Aunt Cynthy Dallett

Sarah Orne Jewett

1

"**N**o," said Mrs. Hand, speaking wistfully,—"no, we never were in the habit of keeping Christmas at our house. Mother died when we were all young; she would have been the one to keep up with all new ideas, but father and grandmother were old-fashioned folks, and—well, you know how 't was then, Miss Pendexter: nobody took much notice of the day except to wish you a Merry Christmas."

"They didn't do much to make it merry, certain," answered Miss Pendexter. "Sometimes nowadays I hear folks complainin' o' bein' overtaxed with all the Christmas work they have to do."

"Well, others think that it makes a lovely chance for all that really enjoys givin'; you get an opportunity to speak your kind feelin' right out," answered Mrs. Hand, with a bright smile. "But there! I shall always keep New Year's Day, too; it won't do no hurt to have an extra day kept an' made pleasant. And there's many of the real old folks have got pretty things to remember about New Year's Day."

"Aunt Cynthy Dallett's just one of 'em," said Miss Pendexter. "She's always very reproachful if I don't get up to see her. Last year I missed it, on account of a light fall o' snow that seemed to make the walkin' too bad, an' she sent a neighbor's boy 'way down from the mount'in to see if I was sick. Her lameness confines her to the house altogether now, an' I have her on my mind a good deal.

How anybody does get thinkin' of those that lives alone, as they get older! I waked up only last night with a start, thinkin' if Aunt Cynthy's house should get afire or anything, what she would do, 'way up there all alone. I was half dreamin', I s'pose, but I couldn't seem to settle down until I got up an' went upstairs to the north garret window to see if I could see any light; but the mountains was all dark an' safe, same's usual. I remember noticin' last time I was there that her chimney needed pointin', and I spoke to her about it,—the bricks looked poor in some places."

"Can you see the house from your north gable window?" asked Mrs. Hand, a little absently.

"Yes'm; it's a great comfort that I can," answered her companion. "I have often wished we were near enough to have her make me some sort o' signal in case she needed help. I used to plead with her to come down and spend the winters with me, but she told me one day I might as well try to fetch down one o' the old hemlocks, an' I believe 't was true."

"Your aunt Dallett is a very self-contained person," observed Mrs. Hand.

"Oh, very!" exclaimed the elderly niece, with a pleased look. "Aunt Cynthy laughs, an' says she expects the time will come when age 'll compel her to have me move up an' take care of her; and last time I was there she looked up real funny, an' says, 'I do' know, Abby; I'm most afeard sometimes that I feel myself beginnin' to look for'ard to it!' 'T was a good deal, comin' from Aunt Cynthy, an' I so esteemed it."

"She ought to have you there now," said Mrs. Hand. "You'd both make a savin' by doin' it; but I don't expect she needs to save as much as some. There! I know just how you both feel. I like to have my own home an' do everything just my way too." And the friends laughed, and looked at each other affectionately.

"There was old Mr. Nathan Dunn,—left no debts an' no money when he died," said Mrs. Hand. "'T was over to his niece's last summer. He had a little money in his wallet, an' when the bill for funeral expenses come in there was just exactly enough; some item or other made it come to so many dollars an' eighty-four cents, and, lo an' behold! there was eighty-four cents in a little separate pocket beside the neat fold o' bills, as if the old gentleman had known beforehand. His niece couldn't help laughin', to save her; she said the old gentleman died as methodical as he lived. She didn't expect he had any money, an' was prepared to pay for everything herself; she's very well off."

"'T was funny, certain,": said Miss Pendexter. "I expect he felt comfortable, knowin' he had that money by him. 'T is a comfort, when all's said and done, 'specially to folks that's gettin' old."

A sad look shadowed her face for an instant, and then she smiled and rose to take leave, looking expectantly at her hostess to see if there were anything more to be said.

"I hope to come out square myself," she said, by way of farewell pleasantry; "but there are times when I feel doubtful."

Mrs. Hand was evidently considering something, and waited a moment or two before she spoke. "Suppose we both walk up to see your aunt Dallett, New Year's Day, if it ain't too windy and the snow keeps off?" she proposed. "I couldn't rise the hill if 't was a windy day. We could take a hearty breakfast an' start in good season; I'd rather walk than ride, the road's so rough this time o' year."

"Oh, what a person you are to think o' things! I did so dread goin' 'way up there all alone," said Abby Pendexter. "I'm no hand to go off alone, an' I had it before me, so I really got to dread it. I do so enjoy it after I get there, seein' Aunt Cynthy, an' she's always so much better than I expect to find her."

"Well, we'll start early," said Mrs. Hand cheerfully; and so they parted. As Miss Pendexter went down the foot-path to the gate, she sent grateful thoughts back to the little sitting-room she had just left.

"How doors are opened!" she exclaimed to herself. "Here I've been so poor an' distressed at beginnin' the year with nothin', as it were, that I couldn't think o' even goin' to make poor old Aunt Cynthy a friendly call. I'll manage to make some kind of a little pleasure too, an' somethin' for dear Mis' Hand. 'Use what you've got,' mother always used to say when every sort of an emergency come up, an' I may only have wishes to give, but I'll make 'em good ones!"

2

The first day of the year was clear and bright, as if it were a New Year's pattern of what winter can be at its very best. The two friends were prepared for changes of weather, and met each other well wrapped in their winter cloaks and shawls, with sufficient brown barge veils tied securely over their bonnets. They ignored for some time the plain truth that each carried something under her arm; the shawls were rounded out suspiciously, especially Miss Pendexter's, but each respected the other's air of secrecy. The narrow road was frozen in deep ruts, but a smooth-trodden little foot-path that ran along its edge was very inviting to the wayfarers. Mrs. Hand walked first and Miss Pendexter followed, and they were talking busily nearly all the way, so that they had to stop for breath now and then at the tops of the little hills. It was not a hard walk; there were a good many almost level stretches through the woods, in spite of the fact that they should be a very great deal higher when they reached Mrs. Dallett's door.

"I do declare, what a nice day 't is, an' such pretty footin'!" said Mrs. Hand, with satisfaction. "Seems to me as if my feet went o' themselves; gener'lly I have to toil so when I walk that I can't enjoy nothin' when I get to a place."

"It's partly this beautiful bracin' air," said Abby Pendexter. "Sometimes such nice air comes just before a fall of snow. Don't it seem to make anybody feel young again and to take all your troubles away?"

Mrs. Hand was a comfortable, well-to-do soul, who seldom worried about anything, but something in her companion's tone touched her heart, and she glanced sidewise and saw a pained look in Abby Pendexter's thin face. It was a moment for confidence.

"Why, you speak as if something distressed your mind, Abby," said the elder woman kindly.

"I ain't one that has myself on my mind as a usual thing, but it does seem now as if I was goin' to have it very hard," said Abby. "Well, I've been anxious before."

"Is it anything wrong about your property?" Mrs. Hand ventured to ask.

"Only that I ain't got any," answered Abby, trying to speak gayly.

"'T was all I could do to pay my last quarter's rent, twelve dollars. I sold my hens, all but this one that had run away at the time, an' now I'm carryin' her up to Aunt Cynthy, roasted just as nice as I know how."

"I thought you was carrying somethin'," said Mrs. Hand, in her usual tone. "For me, I've got a couple o' my mince pies. I thought the old lady might like 'em; one we can eat for dinner, and one she shall have to keep. But weren't you unwise to sacrifice your poultry, Abby? You always need eggs, and hens don't cost much to keep."

"Why, yes, I shall miss 'em," said Abby; "but, you see, I had to do every way to get my rent-money. Now the shop's shut down I haven't got any way of earnin' anything, and I spent what little I've saved through the summer."

"Your aunt Cynthy ought to know it an' ought to help you," said Mrs. Hand. "You're a real foolish person, I must say. I expect you do for her when she ought to do for you."

"She's old, an' she's all the near relation I've got," said the little woman. "I've always felt the time would come when she'd need me, but it's been her great pleasure to live alone an' feel free. I shall get along somehow, but I shall have it hard. Somebody may want help for a spell this winter, but I'm afraid I shall have to give up my house. 'T ain't as if I owned it. I don't know just what to do, but there'll be a way."

Mrs. Hand shifted her two pies to the other arm, and stepped across to the other side of the road where the ground looked a little smoother.

"No, I wouldn't worry if I was you, Abby," she said. "There, I suppose if 't was me I should worry a good deal more! I expect I should lay awake nights." But Abby answered nothing, and they came to a steep place in the road and found another subject for conversation at the top.

"Your aunt don't know we're coming?" asked the chief guest of the occasion.

"Oh, no, I never send her word," said Miss Pendexter. "She'd be so desirous to get everything ready, just as she used to."

"She never seemed to make any trouble o' havin' company; she always appeared so easy and pleasant, and let you set with her while she made her preparations," said Mrs. Hand, with great approval. "Some has such a dreadful way of making you feel inopportune, and you can't always send word you're comin'. I did have a visit once that's always been a lesson to me; 't was years ago; I don't know 's I ever told you?"

"I don't believe you ever did," responded the listener to this somewhat indefinite prelude.

"Well, 't was one hot summer afternoon. I set forth an' took a great long walk 'way over to Mis' Eben Fulham's, on the crossroad between the cranberry ma'sh and Staples's Corner. The doctor was drivin' that way, an' he give me a lift that shortened it some at the last; but I never should have started, if I'd known 't was so far. I had been promisin' all summer to go, and every time I saw Mis' Fulham, Sundays, she'd say somethin' about it. We wa'n't very well acquainted, but always friendly. She moved here from Bedford Hill."

"Oh, yes; I used to know her," said Abby, with interest.

"Well, now, she did give me a beautiful welcome when I got there," continued Mrs. Hand. "'T was about four o'clock in the afternoon, an' I told her I'd come to accept her invitation if 't was convenient, an' the doctor had been called several miles beyond and expected to be detained, but he was goin' to pick me up as he returned about seven; 't was very kind of him. She took me right in, and she did appear so pleased, an' I must go right into the best room where 't was cool, and then she said she'd have tea early, and I should have to excuse her a short time. I asked her not to make any difference, and if I couldn't assist her; but she said no, I must just take her as I found her; and she give me a large fan, and off she went.

"There. I was glad to be still and rest where 't was cool, an' I set there in the rockin'-chair an' enjoyed it for a while, an' I heard her clacking at the oven door out beyond, an' gittin' out some dishes. She was a brisk-actin' little woman, an' I thought I'd caution her when she come back not to make up a great fire, only for a cup o' tea, perhaps. I started to go right out in the kitchen, an' then somethin' told me I'd better not, we never'd been so free together as that; I didn't know how she'd take it, an' there I set an' set. 'T was sort of a greenish light in the best room, an' it begun to feel a little damp to me,—the s'rubs outside grew close up to the windows. Oh, it did seem dreadful long! I could hear her busy with the dishes an' beatin' eggs an' stirrin', an' I knew she was puttin' herself out to get up a great supper, and I kind o' fidgeted about a little an' even stepped to the door, but I thought she'd expect me to remain where I was. I saw everything in that room forty times over, an' I did divert myself killin' off a brood o' moths that was in a worsted-work mat on the table. It all fell to pieces. I never saw such a sight o' moths to once. But occupation failed after that, an' I begun to feel sort o' tired an' numb. There was one o' them late crickets got into the room an' begun to chirp, an' it sounded kind o' fallish. I couldn't help sayin' to myself that Mis' Fulham had forgot all about my bein' there. I thought of all the beauties of hospitality that ever I see!"—

"Didn't she ever come back at all, not whilst things was in the oven, nor nothin'?" inquired Miss Pendexter, with awe.

"I never see her again till she come beamin' to the parlor door an' invited me to walk out to tea," said Mrs. Hand. "'T was 'most a quarter past six by the clock; I thought 't was seven. I'd thought o' everything, an' I'd counted, an' I'd trotted my foot, an' I'd looked more'n twenty times to see if there was any more moth-millers."

"I s'pose you did have a very nice tea?" suggested Abby, with interest.

"Oh, a beautiful tea! She couldn't have done more if I'd been the Queen," said Mrs. Hand. "I don't know how she could ever have done it all in the time, I'm sure. The table was loaded down; there was cup-custards and custard pie, an' cream pie, an' two kinds o' hot biscuits, an' black tea as well as green, an' elegant cake,—one kind she'd just made new, and called it quick cake; I've often made it since—an' she'd opened her best preserves, two kinds. We set down together, an' I'm sure I appreciated what she'd done; but 't wa'n't no time for real conversation whilst we was to the table, and before we got quite through the doctor come hurryin' along, an' I had to leave. He asked us if we'd had a good talk, as we come out, an' I couldn't help laughing to myself; but she said quite hearty that she'd had a nice visit from me. She appeared well satisfied, Mis' Fulham did; but for me, I was disappointed; an' early that fall she died."

Abby Pendexter was laughing like a girl; the speaker's tone had grown more and more complaining. "I do call that a funny experience," she said. "'Better a dinner o' herbs.' I guess that text must ha' risen to your mind in connection. You must tell that to Aunt Cynthy, if conversation seems to fail." And she laughed again, but Mrs. Hand still looked solemn and reproachful.

"Here we are; there's Aunt Cynthy's lane right ahead, there by the great yellow birch," said Abby. "I must say, you've made the way seem very short, Mis' Hand."

3

Old Aunt Cynthia Dallett sat in her high-backed rocking-chair by the little north window, which was her favorite dwelling-place.

"New Year's Day again," she said aloud,—"New Year's Day again!" And she folded her old bent hands, and looked out at the great woodland view and the hills without really seeing them, she was lost in so deep a reverie. "I'm gittin' to be very old," she added, after a little while.

It was perfectly still in the small gray house. Outside in the apple-trees there were some blue-jays flitting about and calling noisily, like schoolboys fighting at their games. The kitchen was full of pale winter sunshine. It was more like late October than the first of January, and the plain little room seemed to smile back into the sun's face. The outer door was standing open into the green dooryard, and a fat small dog lay asleep on the step. A capacious cupboard stood behind Mrs. Dallett's chair and kept the wind away from her corner. Its doors and drawers were painted a clean lead-color, and there were places round the knobs and buttons where the touch of hands had worn deep into the wood. Every braided rug was straight on the floor. The square clock on its shelf between the front windows looked as if it had just had its face washed and been wound up for a whole year to come. If Mrs. Dallett turned

her head she could look into the bedroom, where her plump feather bed was covered with its dark blue homespun winter quilt. It was all very peaceful and comfortable, but it was very lonely. By her side, on a light-stand, lay the religious newspaper of her denomination, and a pair of spectacles whose jointed silver bows looked like a funny two-legged beetle cast helplessly upon its back.

"New Year's Day again," said old Cynthia Dallett. Time had left nobody in her house to wish her a Happy New Year,—she was the last one left in the old nest. "I'm gittin' to be very old," she said for the second time; it seemed to be all there was to say.

She was keeping a careful eye on her friendly clock, but it was hardly past the middle of the morning, and there was no excuse for moving; it was the long hour between the end of her slow morning work and the appointed time for beginning to get dinner. She was so stiff and lame that this hour's rest was usually most welcome, but to-day she sat as if it were Sunday, and did not take up her old shallow splint basket of braiding-rags from the side of her footstool.

"I do hope Abby Pendexter'll make out to git up to see me this afternoon as usual," she continued. "I know 't ain't so easy for her to get up the hill as it used to be, but I do seem to want to see some o' my own folks. I wish 't I'd thought to send her word I expected her when Jabez Hooper went back after he came up here with the flour. I'd like to have had her come prepared to stop two or three days."

A little chickadee perched on the windowsill outside and bobbed his head sideways to look in, and then pecked impatiently at the glass. The old woman laughed at him with childish pleasure and felt companioned; it was pleasant at that moment to see the life in even a bird's bright eye.

"Sign of a stranger," she said, as he whisked his wings and flew away in a hurry. "I must throw out some crumbs for 'em; it's getting to be hard pickin' for the stayin'-birds." She looked past the trees of her little orchard now with seeing eyes, and followed the long forest slopes that led downward to the lowland country. She could see the two white steeples of Fairfield Village, and the map of fields and pastures along the valley beyond, and the great hills across the valley to the westward. The scattered houses looked like toys that had been scattered by children. She knew their lights by night, and watched the smoke of their chimneys by day. Far to the northward were higher mountains, and these were already white with snow. Winter was already in sight, but to-day the wind was in the south, and the snow seemed only part of a great picture.

"I do hope the cold'll keep off a while longer," thought Mrs. Dallett. "I don't know how I'm going to get along after the deep snow comes."

The little dog suddenly waked, as if he had had a bad dream, and after giving a few anxious whines he began to bark outrageously. His mistress tried, as usual, to appeal to his better feelings.

"'T ain't nobody, Tiger," she said. "Can't you have some patience? Maybe it's some foolish boys that's rangin' about with their guns." But Tiger kept on, and even took the trouble to waddle in on his short legs, barking all the way. He looked warningly at her, and then turned and ran out again. Then she saw him go hurrying down to the bars, as if it were an occasion of unusual interest.

"I guess somebody is comin'; he don't act as if 't were a vagrant kind o' noise; must really be somebody in our lane." And Mrs. Dallett smoothed her apron and gave an anxious housekeeper's glance round the kitchen. None of her state visitors, the minister or the deacons, ever came in the morning. Country people are usually too busy to go visiting in the forenoons.

Presently two figures appeared where the road came out of the woods,—the two women already known to the story, but very surprising to Mrs. Dallett; the short, thin one was easily recognized as Abby Pendexter, and the taller, stout one was soon discovered to be Mrs. Hand. Their old friend's heart was in a glow. As the guests approached they could see her pale face with its thin white hair framed under the close black silk handkerchief.

"There she is at her window smilin' away!" exclaimed Mrs. Hand; but by the time they reached the doorstep she stood waiting to meet them.

"Why, you two dear creatur's!" she said, with a beaming smile. "I don't know when I've ever been so glad to see folks comin'. I had a kind of left-all-alone feelin' this mornin', an' I didn't even

make bold to be certain o' you, Abby, though it looked so pleasant. Come right in an' set down. You're all out o' breath, ain't you, Mis' Hand?"

Mrs. Dallett led the way with eager hospitality. She was the tiniest little bent old creature, her handkerchiefed head was quick and alert, and her eyes were bright with excitement and feeling, but the rest of her was much the worse for age; she could hardly move, poor soul, as if she had only a make-believe framework of a body under a shoulder-shawl and thick petticoats. She got back to her chair again, and the guests took off their bonnets in the bedroom, and returned discreet and sedate in their black woolen dresses. The lonely kitchen was blest with society at last, to its mistress's heart's content. They talked as fast as possible about the weather, and how warm it had been walking up the mountain, and how cold it had been a year ago, that day when Abby Pendexter had been kept at home by a snowstorm and missed her visit. "And I ain't seen you now, aunt, since the twenty-eighth of September, but I've thought of you a great deal, and looked forward to comin' more'n usual," she ended, with an affectionate glance at the pleased old face by the window.

"I've been wantin' to see you, dear, and wonderin' how you was gettin' on," said Aunt Cynthy kindly. "And I take it as a great attention to have you come to-day, Mis' Hand," she added, turning again towards the more distinguished guest. "We have to put one thing against another. I should hate dreadfully to live anywhere except on a high hill farm, 'cordin' as I was born an' raised. But there ain't the chance to neighbor that townfolks has, an' I do seem to have more lonely hours than I used to when I was younger. I don't know but I shall soon be gittin' too old to live alone." And she turned to her niece with an expectant, lovely look, and Abby smiled back.

"I often wish I could run in an' see you every day, aunt," she answered. "I have been sayin' so to Mrs. Hand."

"There, how anybody does relish company when they don't have but a little of it!" exclaimed Aunt Cynthia. "I am all alone to-day; there is going to be a shootin'-match somewhere the other side o' the mountain, an' Johnny Foss, that does my chores, begged off to go when he brought the milk unusual early this mornin'. Gener'lly he's about here all the fore part of the day; but he don't go off with the boys very often, and I like to have him have a little sport; 't was New Year's Day, anyway; he's a good, stiddy boy for my wants."

"Why, I wish you Happy New Year, aunt!" said Abby, springing up with unusual spirit. "Why, that's just what we come to say, and we like to have forgot all about it!" She kissed her aunt, and stood a minute holding her hand with a soft, affectionate touch. Mrs. Hand rose and kissed Mrs. Dallett too, and it was a moment of ceremony and deep feeling.

"I always like to keep the day," said the old hostess, as they seated themselves and drew their splint-bottomed chairs a little nearer together than before. "You see, I was brought up to it, and father made a good deal of it; he said he liked to make it pleasant and give the year a fair start. I can see him now, how he used to be standing there by the fireplace when we came out o' the two bedrooms early in the morning, an' he always made out, poor's he was, to give us some little present, and he'd heap 'em up on the corner o' the mantelpiece, an' we'd stand front of him in a row, and mother be bustling about gettin' breakfast. One year he give me a beautiful copy o' the 'Life o' General Lafayette,' in a green cover,—I've got it now, but we child'n 'bout read it to pieces,—an' one year a nice piece o' blue ribbon, an' Abby—that was your mother, Abby—had a pink one. Father was real kind to his child'n. I thought o' them early days when I first waked up this mornin', and I couldn't help lookin' up then to the corner o' the shelf just as I used to look."

"There's nothin' so beautiful as to have a bright childhood to look back to," said Mrs. Hand. "Sometimes I think child'n has too hard a time now,—all the responsibility is put on to 'em, since they take the lead o' what to do an' what they want, and get to be so toppin' an' knowin'. 'T was happier in the old days, when the fathers an' mothers done the rulin'."

"They say things have changed," said Aunt Cynthy; "but staying right here, I don't know much of any world but my own world."

Abby Pendexter did not join in this conversation, but sat in her straight-backed chair with folded hands and the air of a good child.

The little old dog had followed her in, and now lay sound asleep again at her feet. The front breadth of her black dress looked rusty and old in the sunshine that slanted across it, and the aunt's sharp eyes saw this and saw the careful darns. Abby was as neat as wax, but she looked as if the frost had struck her. "I declare, she's gittin' along in years," thought Aunt Cynthia compassionately. "She begins to look sort o' set and dried up, Abby does. She oughtn't to live all alone; she's one that needs company."

At this moment Abby looked up with new interest. "Now, aunt," she said, in her pleasant voice, "I don't want you to forget to tell me if there ain't some sewin' or mendin' I can do whilst I'm here. I know your hands trouble you some, an' I may's well tell you we're bent on stayin' all day an' makin' a good visit, Mis' Hand an' me."

"Thank ye kindly," said the old woman; "I do want a little sewin' done before long, but 't ain't no use to spile a good holiday." Her face took a resolved expression. "I'm goin' to make other arrangements," she said. "No, you needn't come up here to pass New Year's Day an' be put right down to sewin'. I make out to do what mendin' I need, an' to sew on my hooks an' eyes. I get Johnny Ross to thread me up a good lot o' needles every little while, an' that helps me a good deal. Abby, why can't you step into the best room an' bring out the rockin'-chair? I seem to want Mis' Hand to have it."

"I opened the window to let the sun in awhile," said the niece, as she returned. "It felt cool in there an' shut up."

"I thought of doin' it not long before you come," said Mrs. Dallett, looking gratified. Once the taking of such a liberty would have been very provoking to her. "Why, it does seem good to have somebody think o' things an' take right hold like that!"

"I'm sure you would, if you were down at my house," said Abby, blushing. "Aunt Cynthy, I don't suppose you could feel as if 't would be best to come down an' pass the winter with me,—just durin' the cold weather, I mean. You'd see more folks to amuse you, an'—I do think of you so anxious these long winter nights."

There was a terrible silence in the room, and Miss Pendexter felt her heart begin to beat very fast. She did not dare to look at her aunt at first.

Presently the silence was broken. Aunt Cynthia had been gazing out of the window, and she turned towards them a little paler and older than before, and smiling sadly.

"Well, dear, I'll do just as you say," she answered. "I'm beat by age at last, but I've had my own way for eighty-five years, come the month o' March, an' last winter I did use to lay awake an' worry in the long storms. I'm kind o' humble now about livin' alone to what I was once." At this moment a new light shone in her face. "I don't expect you'd be willin' to come up here an' stay till spring,—not if I had Foss's folks stop for you to ride to meetin' every pleasant Sunday, an' take you down to the Corners plenty o' other times besides?" she said beseechingly. "No, Abby, I'm too old to move now; I should be homesick down to the village. If you'll come an' stay with me, all I have shall be yours. Mis' Hand hears me say it."

"Oh, don't you think o' that; you're all I've got near to me in the world, an' I'll come an' welcome," said Abby, though the thought of her own little home gave a hard tug at her heart. "Yes, Aunt Cynthy, I'll come, an' we'll be real comfortable together. I've been lonesome sometimes"—

"'T will be best for both," said Mrs. Hand judicially. And so the great question was settled, and suddenly, without too much excitement, it became a thing of the past.

"We must be thinkin' o' dinner," said Aunt Cynthia gayly. "I wish I was better prepared; but there's nice eggs an' pork an' potatoes, an' you girls can take hold an' help." At this moment the roast chicken and the best mince pies were offered and kindly accepted, and before another hour had gone they were sitting at their New Year feast, which Mrs. Dallett decided to be quite proper for the Queen.

Before the guests departed, when the sun was getting low, Aunt Cynthia called her niece to her side and took hold of her hand.

"Don't you make it too long now, Abby," said she. "I shall be wantin' ye every day till you come; but you mustn't forgit what a set old thing I be."

Abby had the kindest of hearts, and was always longing for somebody to love and care for; her aunt's very age and helplessness seemed to beg for pity.

"This is Saturday; you may expect me the early part of the week;

and thank you, too, aunt," said Abby.

Mrs. Hand stood by with deep sympathy. "It's the proper thing," she announced calmly. "You'd both of you be a sight happier; and truth is, Abby's wild an' reckless, an' needs somebody to stand right over her, Mis' Dallett. I guess she'll try an' behave, but there— there's no knowin'!" And they all laughed. Then the New Year guests said farewell and started off down the mountain road. They looked back more than once to see Aunt Cynthia's face at the window as she watched them out of sight. Miss Abby Pendexter was full of excitement; she looked as happy as a child..

"I feel as if we'd gained the battle of Waterloo," said Mrs. Hand. "I've really had a most beautiful time. You an' your aunt mustn't forgit to invite me up some time again to spend another day."